THE PROFESSIONAL SCHOOL AND WORLD AFFAIRS:

Report of the Task Force on Business Administration
and Public Administration

THE PROFESSIONAL SCHOOL AND WORLD AFFAIRS:

Report of the Task Force on Business Administration
and Public Administration

Committee on the Professional School and World Affairs

T. Keith Glennan, Chairman
Irwin T. Sanders, Study Director

Education and World Affairs
522 Fifth Avenue, New York, N.Y. 10036

CONTENTS

Irwin T. Sanders, Study Director and Peter N.
Gillingham, Associate Study Director

Preface to Study

On the eighth of July, 1965, approximately 30 persons from campuses the nation over came together in Chicago to launch a two-year study, under the aegis of Education and World Affairs, on "the professional school and world affairs." Since that time, these busy men—with commendable diligence—have been concerning themselves with the extent and meaning of the developing interests in world affairs expressed by professional school students and faculty members, as well as by foundations and governmental agencies with overseas commitments, in need of expert professional assistance.

As an outgrowth of that meeting, four task forces were designated, each of which accepted responsibility for the study of two major fields of professional education.

Since the initiation of the study, events related to the field of international education have served to make even more relevant the reports of these four task forces. Perhaps most noteworthy is the International Education Act of 1966, which is concerned with the professional schools as well as the liberal arts. The Act proposes practical steps to remedy the present imbalance between the limited availability of resources within U. S. higher education for international programs and the increased demands being made upon these scarce resources.

The task force reports are appearing in a number of separate volumes. Albert C. Van Dusen, Vice Chancellor for the Professions, the University of Pittsburgh, chaired the Task Force on Business Administration and Public Administration. The report on Agriculture and Engineering was completed under the chairmanship of Paul A. Miller, Assistant Secretary for Education, Department of Health, Education, and Welfare. The report on Medicine and Public Health was prepared under the chairmanship of Mark H. Lepper, M.D., Executive Vice President for Professional and Academic Affairs of the Presbyterian-St. Luke's Hospital, Chicago. The report on Education, directed by John H. Fischer, President of Teachers College, Columbia University and the report on Law, directed by Derek C. Bok, Professor of Law, Harvard University, have been prepared under the general supervision of Edward Levi, Provost, University of Chicago. To these men and their associates in their respective task forces, I express my wholehearted appreciation for the thoughtful way in which they approached their tasks and the diligent manner in which they completed them.

It is a particular pleasure for me to recognize here the effective efforts of the Study Director, Irwin T. Sanders, Vice President of Education and World Affairs. Much credit for the completed study must be given to him and to his able Associate Study Director, Peter N. Gillingham, EWA Executive Associate, as well as to Miss Alice Tetelman, EWA Research Assistant.

T. KEITH GLENNAN
Chairman, Study Committee on the
Professional School and World Affairs

STUDY COMMITTEE

T. Keith Glennan, Chairman   President, Associated Universities, Inc.

Irwin T. Sanders, Study Director   Vice President, Education and World Affairs

Leroy E. Burney, M.D.   Vice President for Health Sciences, Temple University

Paul F. Chenea   Vice President for Academic Affairs, Purdue University

D. W. Colvard   Chancellor, University of North Carolina at Charlotte

John J. Corson   Consultant

John H. Fischer   President, Teachers College, Columbia University

George T. Harrell, Jr., M.D.   Dean, College of Medicine, The Milton S. Hershey Medical Center, The Pennsylvania State University

Alexander Heard   Chancellor, Vanderbilt University

Thomas H. Hunter, M.D.   Chancellor for Medical Affairs, University of Virginia

John B. Howard   President, International Legal Center, New York

Mark H. Lepper, M.D.   Executive Vice President, Professional and Academic Affairs, Presbyterian-St. Luke's Hospital, Chicago

Edward H. Levi   Provost, University of Chicago

Paul A. Miller   Assistant Secretary for Education, Department of Health, Education, and Welfare

Alfred C. Neal   President, Committee for Economic Development

Frank C. Newman   Professor, School of Law, University of California, Berkeley

James A. Perkins   President, Cornell University

Harry H. Ransom   Chancellor, University of Texas

George P. Shultz   Dean, Graduate School of Business, University of Chicago

Albert C. Van Dusen   Vice Chancellor—The Professions, University of Pittsburgh

———————

Eric Larrabee, Special Consultant

Peter N. Gillingham, Associate Study Director   Executive Associate, Education and World Affairs

Alice Tetelman, Research Assistant   Education and World Affairs

9

Introduction to Study

More than two years ago Education and World Affairs (EWA) launched a national study of an important but little examined facet of U. S. professional education: the reciprocal impact between the professional school and international affairs. Several reasons prompted EWA to sponsor this study.

Along with every other aspect of higher education, the professional schools of the United States are going through a period of growth, of ferment and of reexamination. Their relationships to undergraduate education, to the multiversities of which they are part, and to the outside body of professional practitioners are matters of considerable public interest.

As EWA considered the situation, it seemed ironical that—despite what was obviously a heavy involvement of professional schools in the problems of the outside world—there had been no national assessment of current trends and future prospects. It was clear that the need was not primarily to suggest opportunities for overseas work for U. S. professional people, nor to importune the leaders of the professional schools to open their windows on the world.

The Key Role of the Professional Person in Public and International Affairs

What did lead Education and World Affairs to undertake the task, however, was the gap between the reality of professional school involvement in international affairs on the one hand, and the surprising lack of self-awareness and of articulation of purpose and meaning on the other hand. We know only too well what has actually happened—professional people from every field, from medicine and law to social work and education—are prominent in the ranks of "the overseas Americans." But we are not nearly so well informed about the meaning of this involvement for the process of modernization abroad and for the substance of professional education at home.

The professions have developed an international outreach for the simple reason that the functions they serve must be performed in all societies. From the primitive to the most complex and advanced countries, people must still construct buildings, roads, bridges and irrigation systems. They must grow food and process and market it. They must raise health standards and treat illness. They must establish legal systems, and organize and administer government. And of course they must teach the young. An underdeveloped society is one where these functions are performed at low levels of skill, technique and effectiveness. As men become capable of carrying out these tasks more efficiently and economically, the society "develops."

Considering the long history of international concern and involvement for certain professional fields, why has there so far been little self-conscious con-

11

sideration of the significance of this phenomenon? Certainly one explanation is the current disparity between the manpower resources of most professional fields and the accelerating demands of U. S. society for their services. They are literally so busy getting the necessary jobs done here at home that there is neither time nor occasion for them to stand off and consider the meaning for professional education of these relationships with the outside world.

This tendency is reinforced from another direction: professional educators and practitioners often take a rather culture-bound view of their subject matter. With the exception of those in law, theology and one or two other areas, the professional person is likely to assume that the knowledge, skills, and techniques of his field already have a kind of universal validity and applicability. As the question is sometimes put, why should we think it different to build a bridge or install a hydroelectric power system in Nigeria from creating the same type of installation in the Tennessee Valley complex? One thus comes to assume a much-too-easy transferability from one country to another of principles, approaches and techniques. Professional work abroad or the teaching of students from overseas on the campuses of this country is considered simply an extension of activity from the main center of gravity of the profession in the United States. Given this conceptual framework, there is not likely to be much pondering of the deeper meanings that attach to the international involvements of professional education.

So here was a major impulse prompting EWA to launch the present study—the conviction that our own self-understanding as a people and as an educational community would be advanced if we could search out the *significance* and *implications* of what was obviously a high level of professional school activity in international affairs.

But at the same time we were deeply impressed with the likelihood that this study would shed light on various problems in international education that are usually considered in other contexts. Certain major national concerns could best be explored, it seemed, by looking at the role and performance of U. S. professional schools. For example:

> ▶ Well *over 50 percent of our undergraduate students* take their four baccalaureate years in a professional school. Most proposals directed toward the infusion of international studies into the undergraduate curriculum have been advanced chiefly in terms of the liberal arts college. The different and infinitely more complex problems faced by a professional school in moving in the same direction have not been examined.

> ▶ One of the eight professional fields included in the study is that of Education, or teacher training itself. The *preparation of teachers for the nation's elementary and secondary schools* is a main key to the problem of inculcating an understanding of world affairs during the

early years of a child's schooling. The corresponding part of this study was therefore expected to provide new insights into developments and opportunities for giving U. S. youngsters a comprehension of the outside world.

▶ The great majority of *foreign students* who come to U. S. universities, and nearly all of those who come at the graduate level, are here for professional training—in engineering or agriculture or public administration or medicine or some other field. The much-discussed "foreign student problem," therefore, can most realistically be examined within the framework of one or another of the fields of professional education. This important facet of the foreign student problem has not yet been given intensive study, either in general or in any single professional field.

▶ In the case of *overseas operations*—that important new area of institution-building abroad by U. S. universities—it is usually, in the last analysis, a particular professional school rather than the university as a whole that is carrying out such missions. The entire technical assistance effort of U. S. higher education can therefore be most fully understood in terms of the policies and programs of the professional schools in our universities.

▶ Finally, the influence of international involvement on the *relationship of professional schools to the total universities within which they exist* was seen as a significant question that the study would explore. Demands on the professional schools stemming from the world interests of the U. S. constitute added burdens, new responsibilities, and often unique opportunities that significantly influence the development of professional schools within their university homes.

Study is Central to EWA Objectives

This study should be seen against the background of the major objectives of Education and World Affairs itself. EWA was founded as a nonprofit, educational organization in 1962, primarily to assist in strengthening U. S. colleges and universities in their international teaching, research and service activities. One of its chief purposes is to be a source of authoritative and systematic studies focusing on the international side of higher education. The present reports are the latest in a series which was started in 1963 with the examination of *AID and the Universities*, under the chairmanship of John W. Gardner, then president of the Carnegie Corporation of New York.

More particularly, the study of the professional school and world affairs appears as the third in a triad of reports on the involvement of higher education in world affairs. The first two are well known in educational circles. The 1960 report of the Committee on the University and World Affairs (the

Morrill Committee, established by the Ford Foundation) examined the full sweep of university activities and relationships in international affairs and recommended—among other things—the founding of the new organization which became EWA. The 1964 report of the Committee on the College and World Affairs (the Nason Committee, sponsored by the Hazen Foundation) looked more intensively at the place of world affairs and non-Western studies in the undergraduate curriculum, concentrating mainly on the place such studies should have in the liberal arts college. Neither of these reports, nor others that were made during recent years, explored in depth the complex problem of the relationship of professional schools to world affairs.

The timing of the report is most fortunate. It is being published at a moment when it can be read and considered by leaders of professional education as they seek to relate their own schools and programs to the International Education Act of 1966. (It should be noted that the International Education Act specifically includes U. S. professional schools within its terms of reference, opening up for them the possibilities of the same kind of broad, general, institutional support which that Act is designed to provide for U. S. universities and colleges as total institutions.)

Despite the high satisfaction Education and World Affairs feels in seeing this ambitious effort brought to a successful conclusion, the study should not be advanced as something which is all things to all men. There are a number of things which this report *is not*.

— It is *not* the last and definitive word on the subject. The data are suggestive rather than exhaustive. It is the opening up of an important subject, *not* the rendering of a final judgment on the international aspects of U. S. professional education.

— This is *not* a "do it yourself" manual to be used as the blueprint for "internationalizing" any given professional school. The impetus for institutional evaluation, change, and growth must come from within the schools themselves, working with their professions, their universities, and their broader constituencies in the society.

— This report is obviously *not* a survey of all the professions that might properly have been included, but is rather a concentrated look at eight of the centrally important professional fields.

— This study is *not* just a geiger counter survey to pick up and assemble all the "international pieces" to be found throughout the fabric of U. S. professional education. It is not intended to be an encyclopedia on the subject. It is a more focused effort to organize the results of the study around certain meaningful central questions regarding the international aspects of professional education.

— Finally, this report is *not* intended as a blanket exhortation for all and sundry to move into the international field with a vengeance.

Given the resources available and the enormous domestic tasks that our society lays upon its universities and the professional schools within them, enthusiasm must usually be tempered with restraint and circumspection.

If there is any single message which this report does attempt to convey, however, it is the need for professional schools to approach the opportunities for major service on a world scale, with interest, commitment, a sense of the possible, and a dedication to the best traditions of these fields which—because of the universality of the professional function—are inevitably worldwide.

The Organization of the Study

Selection of Professional Fields. The fundamental questions concerning the conduct of the study that had to be answered at the outset were *which* professional fields should be intensively investigated and *how* those fields should be dealt with. The selection of the eight fields to be covered—agriculture, engineering, law, education (teacher training), business administration, public administration, medicine and public health—necessarily involved an arbitrary cutoff point. It was believed, however, that this was a defensible choice inasmuch as these eight areas represented the great majority of both the professional schools of the United States and of the students enrolled in professional education at the graduate and undergraduate levels. At the same time they included long-established fields with proportionately heavy involvement in international affairs.

Had the resources—both human and financial—been available to extend the study, it would have been logical to treat also such professions as journalism, architecture and planning, social work, theology, military affairs and perhaps others. But in reaching the inevitable compromise between desirability and feasibility, it was decided to concentrate attention on the eight fields listed above.

The Task Forces. Perhaps the most important feature of the study plan was the decision to have a single task force assume the responsibility for two professional fields. Here there were several objectives in view. By asking a single group to examine, for example, the fields of agriculture and engineering, and by naming leading representatives of those two professional fields to the task force, it was hoped that a comparative approach could be built into the study from the very outset. It was believed that this arrangement would encourage a continuing discourse throughout the life of the study between professionals of two fairly distinct but related fields, and thereby would result in the transfer of insights and ideas back and forth across the often high barriers separating particular fields. Furthermore, it was thought that this pattern would facilitate the process of moving from an examination of the situation in each type of professional school to the drawing of whatever generalizations and broad conclusions that could be stated concerning "professional education and world affairs" itself.

On the basis of this pattern, the eight fields were paired and task forces were appointed as follows:

> Agriculture and Engineering
> Law and Education (teacher training)
> Business Administration and Public Administration
> Medicine and Public Health

Task force members included not only educators from the various fields but practitioners as well. There was a conscious attempt to invite not simply those individuals who could be identified as already-convinced internationalists, but those who represented the heart of the professions, and were acknowledged and respected leaders of the particular field regardless of their stance and experience with respect to international concerns.

The full list of task force members which appears elsewhere in this document provides eloquent testimony of the willingness of an outstanding group of leaders from these several professional fields to contribute their time, energy, experience, and thought to the carrying out of what proved to be a complex and absorbing task.

The Study Committee and General Direction. Overall responsibility for this effort was vested in a general study committee composed of three persons from each of the four task forces (the task force chairmen, plus one man from each of the two fields) and other members-at-large from the world of higher education. Again, EWA felt that its own assumptions as to the importance of this study were fully verified when such leading figures on the U. S. educational scene as the following agreed to serve as study committee members-at-large:

> Alexander Heard, Chancellor, Vanderbilt University
> John B. Howard, President, International Legal Center
> Thomas H. Hunter, M.D., Chancellor for Medical Affairs, University of
> Virginia
> Alfred C. Neal, President, Committee for Economic Development
> James A. Perkins, President, Cornell University
> Harry H. Ransom, Chancellor, University of Texas

As is always the case with so complex an undertaking, the man who assumed the chairmanship was crucial to the success of the whole endeavor. Here EWA felt that success was assured when T. Keith Glennan, one of its charter trustees, former President of Case Institute of Technology, first Director of the National Aeronautical and Space Administration, and now President of Associated Universities, Inc., agreed to assume this role. As presiding officer, strategist, gentle prodder of the delinquent, persistent needler of the tardy, and good-humored director of a five-ring circus, Keith Glennan deserves great credit for having carried this intricate operation through to completion and publication.

Comparable in importance to the role of the chairman was the functioning of the staff support arrangement. Here again, EWA was exceedingly fortunate when the Ford Foundation agreed to lend the services of Irwin T. Sanders, then Associate Director of its International Training and Research Program, as study director. Virtually all of the characterizations suggested above for Keith Glennan apply with equal force to the performance of Irwin Sanders.

There was established within EWA the Office of the Study Director which—with Mr. Sanders still carrying major responsibilities at the Ford Foundation—was under the day-to-day direction and supervision of Peter N. Gillingham, Executive Associate of EWA, and those who worked with Mr. Sanders and with him: Alice Tetelman, research assistant, Estelle M. Cashman, Patricia T. Moots and Susan Sherman. Eric Larrabee, as a special consultant, has prepared an interpretive statement for the final volume.

As the work proceeded, close liaison was maintained between the Office of the Study Director and each of the four task forces with its own staff support.

The Conduct of the Study

The overall study committee was first convened in July 1965, in Chicago. This meeting was preceded and followed by a comprehensive search of the literature and preparation of full bibliographical reports by the Office of the Study Director at EWA. From that time forward, until the completion of the draft reports in late 1966, most of the actual work was carried on by the task forces themselves. They followed various procedures: further examination and reading of the literature; meetings among themselves; preparation of outlines and tentative memoranda; sending out questionnaires; campus visits to review the situation at certain representative professional schools within their fields and to talk to the leaders of those institutions; and discussions with colleagues at professional meetings. Each task force enjoyed considerable autonomy and was urged to decide for itself the most suitable combination of techniques for its particular fields. As a consequence, the style varied from one task force to another, both in the proportion of campus visits to other investigative methods, and in the emphasis given to one or another facet of the international dimension of its fields.

Even though the academic year 1965-1966 was dominated by the relatively independent work of the task forces, the general study committee did meet in December of 1965 and again the following May for general discussion and review of progress. By the fall of 1966, the first drafts were ready for presentation by the task forces to the general study committee. Draft circulation, discussion and review by the study committee, both as individuals and *in camera*, continued through the winter of 1966-1967, down to its final meeting on February 9, 1967.

The windup of the study and the tidying up of the last details in preparation for publication have been the responsibility of the Study Director, Mr. Sanders (who on January 1, 1967 joined Education and World Affairs as a Vice President), in regular consultation with Chairman Glennan. Editorial work and technical preparation for publication have been under the supervision of EWA's Director of Information and Publications, Allan A. Michie, and its Publications Editor, Mary Ryan.

The Reports and the Final Summary Volume

EWA is now presenting the reports of the eight fields as prepared by the four task forces. Appearing first as a series of five reports—three containing two fields (Agriculture and Engineering, Business Administration and Public Administration, Medicine and Public Health) and two a single field (Education, Law)—the studies are available for quick distribution to a selected number of university administrators, professional school faculty members, university boards of trustees, state and federal legislators and other interested people. It is hoped that they can provide the basis for much constructive discussion within a professional school itself, across professional schools on a given campus, as well as by those outside the university who are interested in sound professional growth.

The five reports will later on be combined into a single volume, which will also include a much more comprehensive statement on "The Professional School Confronts the World" and an interpretive statement by Eric Larrabee on "Internationalism at Issue." Such a volume should prove indispensable to anyone interested in major issues facing higher education in the United States today and should also give much insight into the commonalities and differences among the eight professional fields under study.

Under a Ford Foundation grant, EWA will sponsor a series of regional conferences to provide a forum for discussion of the recommendations of the report and—in some cases—to lead to a much deeper analysis of some of the topics than has been carried out heretofore.

WILLIAM W. MARVEL
President, Education and World Affairs

Foreword to Report

This study outlines the demands which today's world—and the world of the near future—makes upon U. S. higher education in business administration and public administration. It also assesses the extent to which American universities are responding to these requirements and suggests further steps that they should take to fulfill their responsibilities.

Neither U. S. business administration nor U. S. public administration measures up to the classic requirements of a profession. They both can lay claim to the possession of a systematic body of knowledge of substantial intellectual content and to educational programs designed to develop personal skill in the application of this knowledge to specific cases. They also have associations of members interested in the advancement and dissemination of relevant knowledge. But these associations include only a small fraction of the individuals engaged in what might be considered professional practice. Neither these associations nor other bodies prescribe minimum standards of education and competence for entrance to the profession. Nor have generally applicable standards of professional conduct been established, other than the laws and regulations of some public authorities covering the conduct of public officials and civil servants.

Even if only the higher echelons of large organizations are considered, neither field has secured general acceptance of the idea that professional education is a prerequisite to successful performance. In part, this reflects the relatively recent emergence of widespread professional education and, perhaps, the tendency in these fields for practice to outrun both theory and teaching. There appear to be wider differences in concepts and in curricula among the professional schools in each of these fields than are found in most other professions. This may signify that both professions are in a stage of youthful growth; certainly much of their teaching is still in an empirical and evolutionary stage.

Professional education in business administration and public administration originated in U. S. universities and has had its greatest development in this country. Much of its early growth occurred in the years prior to World War II, when the attention of American business and government—and of American education—was focused upon domestic concerns rather than upon world affairs. The international leadership which the United States has accepted since that period has brought far-reaching changes to almost every aspect of American life. But, as this study indicates, the schools which seek to prepare men and women for senior tasks in our business and governmental institutions have been slow to adjust their educational programs to the new dimensions of these professional activities.

This report is the joint product of a Task Force consisting of:

Stephen K. Bailey, Dean, Maxwell Graduate School of Citizenship and Public Affairs, Syracuse University

Robert C. Calkins, President, The Brookings Institution

John J. Corson, Consultant

C. Jackson Grayson, Jr., Dean, School of Business Administration, Tulane University

Henry Reining, Jr., Dean, School of Public Administration, University of Southern California

Alvin Roseman, Associate Dean, Graduate School of Public and International Affairs, University of Pittsburgh

George P. Shultz, Dean, Graduate School of Business, University of Chicago

Ralph H. Smuckler, Acting Dean of International Programs, Michigan State University

A. C. Van Dusen, Vice Chancellor—The Professions, University of Pittsburgh, Task Force Chairman

The Task Force met five times as a group during the period from July 1965 to September 1966. Campus visits were made by members of the Task Force to the following schools as part of this study:

Northwestern University, School of Business

Cornell University, School of Business and Public Administration

University of Michigan, Institute of Public Administration

State University of New York, School of Public Administration

Princeton University, Woodrow Wilson School of Public and International Affairs

Carnegie Institute of Technology, Graduate School of Industrial Administration

A questionnaire intended to elicit information concerning the world affairs activities of schools which were not known or visited by members of the Task Force was sent to all 120 members of the American Association of Collegiate Schools of Business and to all 68 members of the Council on Graduate Education for Public Administration. The returns from the questionnaire were incomplete. Only 55 business schools and 20 schools of public administration responded to this inquiry. To remedy this deficiency, additional information was secured by telephone interviews with deans and key faculty members of a large number of schools in both fields.

As the Chairman of this Task Force, I wish to express the group's appreciation for the assistance it received from the American Association of Collegiate Schools of Business and from the Council on Graduate Education for Public Administration, and for the cooperation of the administrators and faculty members of many universities and professional schools who responded to requests for information and contributed their experience and suggestions to the preparation of the report.

Members of the Task Force also drew upon their experience at their home campuses, their prior knowledge of certain other institutions, and their consultations with administrative and faculty members of other universities and with leaders of professional associations of the two professional fields.

The members of this group collaborated actively in the development of the report. I wish to thank them, and the several special consultants, for their effective contributions to this common effort.

A. C. VAN DUSEN
Chairman, Task Force on Business Administration and
Public Administration

GENERAL INTRODUCTION AND RECOMMENDATIONS

The future managers of public and private enterprises in America and abroad will live in a world characterized by five essential features:

(1) An unprecedented speed of international communications and transportation. Three-thousand mile an hour air travel and virtually instantaneous telecommunications via satellite will increase geometrically the possibilities, realities, and necessities of international and intercontinental organization—public and private;

(2) A world population explosion, especially in unstable, developing areas, which will create both hopeful and catastrophic possibilities for the entire human race;

(3) Continuing and rising intranational and international political tensions which will have the most profound effect upon the economy and the security of nations;

(4) An increasingly pragmatic, technological, and experimental approach to decision-making within and among nations, with less attention to traditional ideological formulae and greater emphasis upon managerial capabilities;

(5) An increasingly mobile world population—responding to individual, institutional, and political demands for skilled and educated professional manpower.

This environment will condition all human activity, but it will especially affect, and will especially be affected by, professional leaders in business and in public administration.

It is true that most businessmen and most public administrators are not products of professional schools of business administration or of public administration. But these centers of professional learning have an increasingly important role in shaping the ethic and in establishing standards and techniques of performance for the vast and kaleidoscopic activities which comprise the worlds of business and government. Increasingly, the best products of these professional schools are playing key roles in the society:

—They are managing major governmental and business institutions;
—They are becoming important opinion leaders in their communities and in their proliferating professional organizations;

23

—They are shaping the future of professional education in their respective fields and are influencing the development of professional education in other fields;

—They are conducting research on problems central to the administrative concerns of government and business, both domestic and international;

—They are engaging in professional roles and practices which influence, and which are increasingly being influenced by, international forces;

—They are being tapped directly by political decision-makers in the determination of future public policy, including international public policy.

What happens in the general and professional education of business and public administrators is, therefore, significant to the capacity of the human race to deal with the stresses of the last third of the twentieth century. General education in elementary, secondary, and higher institutions of learning has a necessary and important role to play in the professional and civic development of business managers and public administrators. But by definition, general education cannot be expected to dwell on those issues which relate a profession as a profession to the larger context in which its practitioners must function.

It is the central theme of this report that professional schools of business and public administration have failed to face fully the international aspects of their professional responsibilities; that they have defined professional competence too narrowly. In consequence, most of their graduates are not adequately equipped to perform the leadership roles outlined or implied above.

Common Difficulties in Internationalizing Professional Education

The professional schools and programs of business and public administration face common problems in attempting to create or to extend an international component in professional education. These difficulties may be put in the form of questions:

—What is the intellectual content of the needed international component? In practical terms, how can professional schools broaden their sense of relevance and affect the sensitivity of students toward the world around them without diluting the quality of education in the skills which give particular substance to the term "professional?"

—What complexion or "mix" would best enable professional education to meet national and local, as well as international needs?

—How large and extensive should the international component of professional education be?

—Is there sufficient talent and knowledge available to develop meaningful international innovations? Should all teachers be expected to include an international aspect in all courses? If so, how can instructors best be encouraged to do so? Should a single international course be devised and required? If so, what should be its subject matter? Should every professional school have a few optional courses in world affairs, or in specialized fields like international marketing, international administration, comparative commercial law, comparative administration, or international trade and finance?

—Does "internationalizing" imply the development or extension of student and faculty exchanges with other nations?

—Does "internationalizing" imply that professional schools should undertake overseas technical assistance responsibilities under either government or foundation auspices? What advantages are derived from this type of activity? How disruptive of continuing responsibilities for professional education at home are such ventures likely to be?

—Who on the university campus should assume responsibility for infusing a new international component into the professional schools and into the institution's total academic program? How should such effort be organized and administered?

—Does the professional school have a responsibility for mid-career education of an international character to those presently practicing in the respective professional fields?

—Who will finance innovations in curricula, research, staff, and facilities aimed at developing the international component of professional schools in business and public administration?

These questions are suggestive rather than definitive, but they are real and they are difficult. They face every professional school which looks seriously at the issue. Each of them involves costs as well as benefits; every commitment requires reallocation of existing faculty, money, and other resources or the securing of additional means. These problems cannot be resolved by the prose of a report. They will be overcome in different ways by courageous and creative initiative in the variegated schools and universities which—despite their disparate contexts—face in common the insistent demands of the future.

This report attempts no theology of internationalization for professional education in business administration and public administration. It does attempt to present options in the light of existing knowledge and experience, and does press for immediate and dedicated efforts on the part of every professional school of business and of public administration in the nation to measure the adequacy of its existing commitment to the international aspects of professional education against the perceptible and urgent needs of the future.

Some Common Elements of the Two Professional Fields

Professional education in business administration and in public administration deals with different environments. Each has its own concepts and areas of technical knowledge. But they share a number of broad concerns, such as the theory and practice of management; in the international field they have a special interest in the economic development of low-income countries. They also face somewhat similar problems of relationships with other parts of their parent universities.

Management

Both business and government have a common interest in management, especially in methods of determining goals and strategies, techniques of programming, executing and controlling activities, and problems of functioning through complex, large-scale organization. Despite the differences in purposes, in legal status and in operating conditions, the similarities in the underlying management questions have led to joint approaches in professional education for management, especially in connection with such subjects as organizational theory, individual and group behavior, systems analysis, and the application of quantitative methodologies.

In the international aspects of business administration and public administration these common management concerns are reflected in the search for solutions to the difficulties of delegation and communication in geographically far-flung organizations. Both fields require staff capable of dealing with foreign systems that have their roots in other cultures, and in some cases, in other values. Business and governmental personnel stationed abroad must be able to adapt themselves to unfamiliar overseas working and living conditions.

A variety of methods have been employed by schools of business administration and schools of public administration to provide instruction and encourage research in these areas of mutual interest. Several universities have established schools which encompass both fields in their curricula; steps have been taken in several other institutions to include in this combination some of the other specialized areas of administration such as educational administration and hospital administration. Other efforts have involved the development of management courses given collaboratively by the faculties of the two schools, joint appointments for faculty members of one school to enable them to teach management subjects in the other, and the creation of management or administrative science centers as cluster organizations which serve all parts of the university interested in management. The great increase in the use of quantitative methods in both business and public administration, and the obvious advantage of coordinated teaching and use of computer equipment, have stimulated joint activities in this specialization.

There appears to have been less interest in developing joint approaches to the special international aspects of management. This may be attributable to differences in the extent of international interest as between the business administration and the public administration schools within a university. It may also reflect the relatively recent development of international administration as a field of research and teaching.

Economic Development

Economic development of low-income countries is an area of teaching, research, and advisory service that involves a substantial comingling of public administration and business administration, along with a number of other professional and disciplinary fields. Characteristically, these countries lack the institutions and the trained manpower required for both the governmental and the private business activities involved in economic growth. The formulation and execution of national development plans which allocate scarce resources between the public and private sectors demand a sophisticated understanding of the interrelationships between business and government. The regulation of foreign investment, the operation of governmental enterprises of an industrial nature, and the encouragement of an indigenous entrepreneurial community are examples of other aspects of economic development which call for common understanding between public administrators and business administrators.

Those schools of public administration which offer programs of development administration have incorporated courses in development economics and development planning in their curricula. Some of these programs also include courses in the operation of government-owned business enterprises.

Business administration schools do not appear to have added coursework in economic development to their programs as extensively as have their public administration associates. However, in many universities, departments of economics offer such courses in which business administration students may enroll.

There appear to be few examples of collaboration between the two schools of administration to maximize their common knowledge and teaching capabilities in economic development. U. S. and foreign students may study in one of the two schools with little opportunity to appreciate the extent to which the two fields of activity are interrelated in low-income countries. Even in the schools which include both business and public administration in their programs, there is little integrated focus upon the problems of development.

Relationships Within the University

Because the organizational arrangements for both business administration and public administration in U. S. universities range from autonomous graduate professional schools to undergraduate programs in basic disciplinary departments, the problems of relationships within the university structure differ greatly.

The programs established within departments (usually within economics departments for business administration and within political science departments for public administration) often suffer from the attitudes of disciplinary-minded colleagues who sometimes regard these two fields as somewhat illegitimate vocationalism which diverts students from the goals of liberal education. When these departments also include graduate courses in business or public administration, the emphasis usually is placed upon the academic rather than upon the professional aspects of graduate work.

The autonomous or "semi-autonomous" professional schools have much more freedom to develop their curricula to meet their own concepts of professional preparation. They normally are headed by individuals who identify themselves with the application of professional knowledge, and their faculties usually contain a substantial proportion of individuals who have both academic qualifications and practical experience. In general, schools of this type are more innovative and more interested in maintaining a two-way relationship with the world outside the campus than are programs within academic departments.

A third form of organization is that of a "center" which offers courses in a professional field, but which relies primarily for instructors upon faculty members drawn from other schools and academic departments. This arrangement may serve as an effective method for focusing interest of a number of faculty and facilitating interprofessional and professional-disciplinary collaboration. However, it appears more appropriate for continuing education and for work at the doctorate level than for the preparation of practitioners.

While autonomous professional schools have many advantages in the development of their programs, they normally do not include within their own curricula the full range of expertise required for teaching and research in the international aspects of their professions. Through joint faculty appointments or other methods, they must bring to their students the contribution of other parts of the university, especially those of the social sciences. For students who wish to prepare themselves for internationally related work, language and area study in other schools or departments may be especially significant.

The problem of coordination of the various international interests of a university has been the subject of several studies. In almost any form of organization which an institution develops for this purpose, it is probable that professional schools will play a significant role, because on the whole they are "action-minded" and are called upon for assistance by governmental agencies and foundations concerned with the development of the professional and technical manpower resources of overseas countries.

Like the university as a whole, the underlying problem which schools of business and public administration face is that of how they can secure the maximum value from—and make their maximum contribution to—the opportunities for overseas involvement without endangering the performance of their basic responsibility for the education of the students on their home campus.

General Suggestions

Each school of business administration and each school of public administration has its own characteristics and aspirations. Each must determine its own goals and develop its strategy for attaining its institutional objectives. The level of interest in the world affairs aspects of professional education will differ from school to school; so will the resources available, or obtainable, for the international elements of their programs. But there are also significant similarities in the steps to be taken by schools in both fields which decide to move forward with their international content, at a minimal, an intermediate, or an advanced level of world affairs involvement.

Within this broad spread of interests and capabilities, the Task Force believes that some general suggestions can be made to schools in both fields which contemplate the development or enlargement of the international content of their activities:

1. *Every school must develop a conscious strategy concerning the nature, extent, and timing of its involvement in teaching, research, and service activities of an international character.*

2. *The concept of professional education in these two fields requires that every school should have at least a minimal world affairs content in its curriculum and in other aspects of its institutional activity. Beyond this minimum, there is a wide range of measures —involving curricula, faculty development, research activities, technical assistance undertakings, foreign students and overseas internships, and continuing education programs—which require increasingly heavy commitment of faculty and other resources.*

3. *At the minimal level, all schools should:*
   —introduce the international dimension into the basic courses in economics (e.g., balance of payments problems) and government (e.g., impact of foreign relations);
   —sponsor periodic special lectures by scholars or practitioners with

*special knowledge of international problems of professional con-
cern;*

*—encourage students to enroll in relevant international courses
offered in other parts of the university;*

*—stimulate selected faculty members to seek opportunities for
broadening their knowledge of the international aspects of their
specializations;*

*—accept a limited number of qualified foreign students and faculty
members of foreign institutions for study in the school's regular
academic program; and*

*—increase opportunities for the development of the foreign lan-
guage capabilities of both students and faculty.*

4. *Some schools will have both the desire and the capability for going
beyond this minimal level, without committing themselves to the
development of a major emphasis in the international aspects of
professional education. Some of the additional activities which
might be considered by schools at this intermediate level of involvement include:*

*—introducing comparative, cross-cultural and other international
materials into a substantial proportion of existing courses;*

*—initiating a limited number of new courses of specialized inter-
national character;*

*—supporting faculty research of an international nature, including
research designed to enhance faculty competence to use internationally focused materials in present or new courses;*

—increasing the world affairs content of the school's library.

5. *Schools which wish to develop a special institutional competence in
the world affairs aspects of their profession must be prepared to
devote substantial resources to the international area. This level of
involvement is appropriate only for a limited number of schools
which have, or can secure, substantial funds for this purpose. The
spectrum of international activities which such a school might
undertake is both broad and deep. Among them, in addition to the
steps previously mentioned, are:*

*—developing internationally focused courses to prepare students
who wish to specialize in this aspect of their professional field;*

*—systematically incorporating international content in all, or most,
basic professional courses;*

*—recruiting and developing faculty with strong international back-
grounds and maintaining programs for the development of the
international capability of junior faculty;*

*—operating in-service training programs on international problems
for U.S. practitioners;*

—*offering short-term institutes or similar training to non-Americans;*

—*undertaking internationally focused research, including that involved in the development of cases and other teaching materials;*

—*maintaining a program for disseminating research findings and other new knowledge concerning the international aspects of professional education; and*

—*undertaking technical assistance projects for the development of professional education in overseas countries.*

A number of the leading schools of business administration and of public administration have made substantial progress beyond the minimal level and a few are developing a high level of specialized international competence. But the vast majority of schools have taken only limited steps in this direction and some have been almost unmindful of the world affairs dimensions of professional education. The institutions which have incorporated significant international content in their curricula and are engaging in other international activities still have a long and difficult road ahead before they reach a sound balance of domestic and international emphasis. Nevertheless, they have broken through the barriers of culture-bound inertia and are responding to the longer-range needs of their students and of the educational community of which they are an important element.

The schools which have not yet faced up to the world affairs aspects of their educational programs enroll a high proportion of students in the two fields. The faculties, administrators, trustees, and alumni of these institutions have a special responsibility for developing appreciation of the role of these professions in the world of today and of tomorrow. It is upon them that the obligation lies for accelerating the process of institutional change.

BUSINESS SCHOOLS AND EDUCATION FOR INTERNATIONAL BUSINESS*

The International Dimension

U.S. Business Expansion Abroad

The past two decades have witnessed phenomenal growth in the international operations of U. S. business firms. Following World War II, U. S. business expanded overseas operations especially to penetrate the fast-growing European markets. In countries where only foreign marketing activities had been maintained in preexpansion years, U. S. business began to invest heavily in production and transportation facilities. Networks of subsidiaries were created, requiring in many cases a full complement of managerial talent. The rate of expansion accelerated with the emergence of the common market communities in Europe in the late 1950s and early 1960s. Markets opened in Africa and parts of Asia as former colonies and dependencies became independent.

By the mid-1960s, several thousand U. S. corporations had foreign subsidiaries, tens of thousands of U. S. citizens were employed overseas, and more than $45 billion had been invested abroad by U. S. business. While this revolution did not uniformly transform the organizational structures of all internationally minded corporations into "multinational" proportions, it has nonetheless produced a trend toward *international balance* in organizations that had until then been domestic units with a few foreign appendages. U. S. business was, in many instances, reproducing itself abroad. Not surprisingly, the word "foreign" was replaced by "international" or "multinational" in describing such ventures.

Problems of Transition

In aggressively pursuing international markets, U. S. corporations (as well as partnerships in such fields as public accounting) were thrust into political, social, cultural, and commercial milieus that were at once strange and frustrating to U. S. managers accustomed to home conditions. To meet this set of challenges, managers designed a variety of strategies, ranging from the stubborn refusal to abandon U. S. business practices in dealings abroad, to the establishment of elaborate programs aimed at discovering, understanding,

* Prepared with the special assistance of Professor Stephen A. Zeff.

and adapting to the new environments. Novel problems of other sorts called for still further strategies. Global logistics, personnel problems for Americans and foreign nationals, production planning, financial planning and profit-retrieval problems, diverse and uncertain tax laws, problems of form of ownership and extent of ownership by foreign nationals—all these uniquely international problem areas—in addition to the omnipresence of a strange environment—have challenged managers to devise fresh strategies apart from those that may have solved purely domestic problems in the past.

Whether one views this "international revolution" as having caused a "fundamental" change in the way business is done, or as having brought about only a "structural" change in business operations, the transition has been dramatic. It continues, and its future course is little better known today than it was ten years ago. It is in response to this concentrated international expansion of previously domestic enterprise that business schools are struggling to find their own solutions.

The Implications for Business Education

The rapid internationalization of U. S. firms did not go unmarked in U. S. schools of business. In the 1950s, deans and faculties began to discuss with increasing urgency the implications for education. It seemed clear that the business schools, and particularly those in leadership positions, needed to formulate and initiate programs of education and research in the international area. However, massive problems attended this new orientation—problems of designing and integrating new fields into existing curricula, of obtaining or reorienting qualified and interested faculty, of formulating directions and gaining support for research, of designing and supporting extracurricular efforts to link the business schools more closely with this large and emerging need, and above all, of stretching resources to encompass the new assignment.

It was to these problems and their implications that this Task Force addressed itself. Beyond the basic question of what business schools *should* and *can* do in the area of international business without subverting their basic goals, the Task Force sought to develop information in answer to these questions:

(1) *What have been the experiences of schools which entered the international field, and what may be learned from them?*

(2) *What possible strategies may be employed by business schools seeking to expand into this field at various levels of commitment?*

This report provides some approaches to these questions.

The Search for Strategies

The U. S. business school today possesses some of the characteristics of its own product—the burdened, harried business executive. Aggressive, growing in stature and affluence, over-extended in its commitments, the business school faces yet another demand for its attention and resources in the international dimension.

For several reasons, awareness of the need for an expanded effort in the international area has not been matched by action:

(1) Business schools are already taxed with many competing assignments—the preparation of young men in both undergraduate and graduate programs for careers in business, the development of teachers, adult education, executive development programs, and the rapidly expanding research component. The adoption of international programs would require substantial investments of academic manpower and financial resources, now fully committed elsewhere.

(2) Many schools hesitate to venture into international programs because they believe that basic research approaches, a conceptual framework, and sound teaching materials are still lacking.

(3) There is still no clear understanding of just what international business encompasses. Does it mean something more to business schools than material in the traditional courses in international economics and international trade—such as comparative advantage, foreign exchange, balance of payments, commercial treaties —usually offered in the department of economics? (Prior to the 1950s, and especially prior to World War II, "international" did indeed connote little more than the *foreign* operations of a *domestic* company through its import-export arm. To some business schools, this warranted a course in marketing or import-export documentation—the company's major activity abroad.)

(4) Many faculties and deans understandably prefer to continue to focus on U. S. business problems, or on the fields of business (in domestic terms) to which they have devoted themselves in the past—finance, marketing, industrial relations, production—rather than retool for the new assignment.

Few schools have developed carefully studied and well-designed plans for international aspects of their programs. Some schools have accepted tempting offers to enter into partial programs, only to encounter unforeseen difficulties in terms of inadequate budgets, faculty who refuse overseas assignments, language incapacities, lack of integration of the program into the normal curriculum, and thinly conceptualized objectives. Some have organized full-scale "international programs" with numbers of courses labeled "International XXXX" and a faculty with vaccinated arms and current passports. A few have carefully explored alternatives and are cautiously adding international aspects to different parts of their varied programs.

Though responses to the international tug have varied, the genuine concern has not. Hardly a dean or a faculty of business administration is not presently searching for some way to accept this recognized responsibility without diverting purpose or courting bankruptcy.

Thus the central question becomes: What strategies for involvement are worthwhile and workable?

A threshold decision must be faced by any school, even though its ambitions in the international direction are severely limited. In such a case, the questions are: Is there some minimum exposure to the international dimension of business operations that should be acquired by all students and faculty? If so, in what ways may this limited objective be accomplished?

Beyond this threshold lie a great variety of possible strategies involving different levels of commitment along the following lines:

(1) Encouragement of research on international aspects of business operations, often carrying a strong comparative flavor. Such a research effort would almost necessarily be accompanied by courses of study on various aspects of international business operations.

(2) Efforts to facilitate professional work abroad by faculty members.

(3) Encouragement of foreign students to study at the U. S. institution, with an effort to provide reciprocal study and work opportunities abroad for U. S. nationals.

(4) Development of structured and formal arrangements with one or more educational institutions abroad to effect a research base, student exchange, and general institutional development at both ends.

(5) Development of programs for management personnel already active in international operations for their companies.

(6) Organization of a separate and formal specialty in international business as an alternative curriculum paralleling the more general offering.

While answers are not available for all the questions implied by these possibilities, this Task Force has examined possible strategies and has attempted to furnish guidelines and recommendations for interested parties. In considering these, each school will necessarily be conscious of its peculiar comparative advantages, opportunities, objectives and limitations. The strategy it adopts will be related to its own history. Similarly, the variety of strategies emerging in collegiate education for business more generally will be related to the recent developments in this field.

After examining recent developments in business education and relating those developments to international strategy, the report will describe the current scene, and then seek to illuminate the issues in deciding on any particular strategy for involvement.

Recent Developments in Business Education

To place the international business decision in the context of the total business school setting, it is helpful briefly to recapitulate the most important developments in the recent history of higher education for business in the United States.

1. The development of master's and doctor's programs in business has accelerated sharply in recent years. Beginning in 1900 with Dartmouth and continuing with Harvard (1908), Stanford (1925), Cornell (1946), and Carnegie Tech (1949), graduate business schools were created where no business programs had existed before. But starting in the 1940s with Chicago, schools previously giving undergraduate and graduate work became solely graduate schools. Among those that followed are Columbia (1949), Pittsburgh (1961), and—in the mid-1960s—Tulane, UCLA and Northwestern.

Complementing this trend has been the strengthening and broadening of master's programs at schools that continue to offer undergraduate work.[1] Where specialized Master of Science programs were at one time structured upon equally specialized Bachelor of Science programs, today scores of schools offer the generally more analytical Master of Business Administration degree. Even at the undergraduate level, less specialization is evident.

Doctoral programs are offered today at more than 50 business schools, compared to only a handful prior to World War II.

This decisive trend toward master's and doctor's programs has greatly increased the emphasis on scholarly research in the professional lives of business educators. Thus, discussions of new curricular developments, such as education for international business, must consider the implications for research as well as teaching.

2. Both a cause and effect of the movement toward graduate education for business is the fact that business schools have become increasingly attractive to top quality faculty and students. Businesses, recognizing this development, have more eagerly recruited business school graduates for challenging positions, and have engaged faculty members in a growing number of consultative capacities. Hence, as both business school graduates and faculty members become more intimately involved with the problems of middle- and upper-level management, business schools must become more concerned with the managerial and operational changes brought about by the expansion of business into the international sphere.

3. As a result of the two trends just described, the programs directed at producing the flow of teachers and researchers in business and economics will expand. In 1961-62, only 218 Doctor of Philosophy and Doctor of Business Administration degrees were granted in business schools. In two years, the

figure grew to 302, and in 1965-66 it rose sharply to 478. But in the four intervening years, the number of students enrolled in collegiate business programs had grown by scores of thousands. In 1954, the American Association of Collegiate Schools of Business saw the need for an annual output of more than 500 new holders of Doctor's degrees by 1965 to allow for replacement and expansion in collegiate business schools and departments of business.[2] Most observers now believe that this projection is low. The need for teachers and researchers undoubtedly will continue to exceed their production.

4. Among students who matriculate in graduate business programs there is a decided increase in the number whose undergraduate work was in engineering, mathematics or the social sciences, and who bring a stronger technical or conceptual base on which to build the business curriculum. Consequently, graduate business schools are able to develop in students a competence in the applications to business decision-making of quantitative methods and behavioral sciences, without undertaking to teach elementary work in the underlying technical fields and disciplines. In the international sphere, where managers must have a knowledge drawn from many fields and disciplines, this trend is especially welcome.

5. A firmer conceptual base is emerging in business schools, as educators recognize that their comparative advantages lie in the transmission of the scientific knowledge underlying all business, and not in instruction in the past and current practices of business. By teaching such basic disciplines as mathematics, statistics, accounting, economics, law, psychology and sociology, business schools can lay the foundations for subsequent teaching of the operational aspects of business. In an academic setting, current business practices can only be taught vicariously; universities and colleges have the least competence in these areas. Conversely, business is poorly equipped to teach underlying scientific knowledge, but is well equipped to teach business practices.

6. The behavioral sciences have become more important in the business school curriculum, and this trend is likely to accelerate. Research and teaching in the behavioral areas hold great promise for the more effective management of business enterprise, and undoubtedly will contribute to a fuller understanding of organizations, their activities and goals—transcending purely marketing or industrial relations applications. In studying international business, the fields of anthropology, sociology, and psychology are among the keys to understanding and adapting to different social and cultural environments.

7. The growing use of mathematics and statistics in the business-decision process, and the growing applications of computer technology to business management, are reflected in the curricula and research at leading business schools. This development has progressed more rapidly in the United States than in most other countries; nonetheless, it will eventually permeate all decision-making environments, in the United States and abroad.

8. The impact of governmental policies and actions increasingly has come under study in business schools, with impetus furnished by the growing role of government. The attitudes of government toward business in countries abroad are particularly germane in the study of international business.

9. Greater attention is being paid by business to university programs of continuing education for executives. We can expect that such programs will become even more important as the international involvement of business grows and as business school faculties develop their competence, through research, in international business.

While the business of business schools in the United States is undergoing the traumas of self-examination and change, the business-school concept is gaining acceptance abroad. In Great Britain, the combined effect of two significant reports, the Robbins report[3] and the Franks report,[4] was the establishment of two major graduate schools of business; these reports also called for an expansion of business studies in other universities and scientific and technological institutions. Also stressed was the need to create a number of centers for courses in management for persons well along in their business careers.[5]

Antedating these developments in Britain have been the successful attempts to found business schools in Turkey, Brazil, Nigeria, India, the Philippines, Mexico, Canada, Switzerland and France (among others), where schools and institutes have, in many instances, patterned their educational programs for business after the style of business schools in the United States. Hence, these developments—which affect both the international and domestic aspects of business curricula—may soon be felt abroad as keenly as they have been felt here.

We turn now to a survey of international business programs presently being offered by U. S. business schools.

International Business Programs in U. S. Business Schools—A Survey

A survey of some of the current programs in international business at the master's level can best illustrate the range of alternatives available to a business school. The activities comprising international business programs may be grouped under five headings: 1) curriculum, 2) student exchange, 3) research, 4) technical assistance, 5) continuing education.

A survey limited to programs at the master's level reveals the diversity of programs in terms of these five groupings and the diversity of approaches within each grouping.

Curriculum[6]

It is never easy to compare the curricula of different schools. The situation at each school is unique. Decisions on curricula are explicitly or implicitly influenced by objectives, resources, type of student body, location, and myriad other factors. The meaning of words appearing in course titles and even in course descriptions tends to vary from school to school. Such interschool comparisons, moreover, are particularly difficult when they relate—as with international business—to a new area of study.

Essentially we found three types of curricula involving international content:

a. curricula containing at least several courses in international business, leading to a major or concentration;
b. curricula containing several courses in international business, but with no major or concentration;
c. curricula containing very few courses in international business.

In addition, the curricula at some schools contain substantial international content in a number of courses with labels other than "international."

a. At least several courses and a major. Among the schools offering a major or concentration in international business are San Francisco State College, the City College of the City University of New York (CCNY), Indiana University, Cornell University, American University, University of Alabama, Columbia University and Harvard University. Of the eight schools, San Francisco State and CCNY offer the most courses in international business; the six other schools give a half dozen or fewer such courses.

At San Francisco State, undergraduates and graduates may choose from 27 courses[7] offered through the Center for World Business, which is part of the School of Business. Unique among business schools, the School requires Principles of World Trade for *all* M.B.A. students.

CCNY offers majors at both the undergraduate and graduate levels. In both the CCNY undergraduate and graduate catalogs, the international business courses are grouped in the marketing department, a legacy of the origins of the teaching of international work. CCNY offers several "international" courses through functional departments;[8] in addition, it lists 16 courses under "international trade" (undergraduate) and 9 under "international business" (graduate).[9] While full-time faculty members staff the courses at San Francisco State, the entire CCNY international business curriculum is taught by part-time faculty who occupy responsible positions in the international operations of New York-based corporations. The undergraduate and graduate majors at both schools are built on a core common to all functional majors, e.g., accounting, marketing, industrial relations and finance.

In addition to courses in international business, students in all schools in this "major" category take international courses within the functional fields and courses in other disciplines (mainly for environmental studies and languages). Moreover, international topics are integrated in a variety of existing courses. Indiana, for example, limits the peculiarly international business courses to area studies and comparative systems. The functional fields, the department of economics, and other university departments cooperate through an International Business Administration faculty committee in the administration of the program. Faculty in the Indiana Graduate School of Business also offer courses in the university's Latin American Studies Program.

Cornell's Graduate School of Business and Public Administration, in addition to its international business major, also offers a major in international development. Hence, students enrolled in either international business or international development majors are able to combine their interests in both fields when designing their course programs.

As part of its undergraduate and graduate programs, American University has developed an International Business Research Laboratory. Some 200 companies cooperate by sending materials of an international nature, e.g., speeches, market surveys, examples of brands and packaging techniques used in different countries, which are microfilmed and used by students and faculty as a research tool. Roughly paralleling the situation at San Francisco State, a course in Fundamentals of International Business is taken by most undergraduate business majors as part of the core work. American University has a distinct advantage in its location, because embassies in Washington provide quite a number of part-time students for the school's international business program.

Although Columbia and Harvard offer a major or concentration in international business, this is for administrative convenience and not because they believe that international business qualifies as a separate and distinct field of study. It is anticipated that this major might be dropped when it becomes practicable to integrate international aspects into the functional fields.

The program at Columbia underscores both international development and international enterprise. The some half-dozen courses offered under the heading of "international business" are intended to give a foundation to all students interested in international business. Some international work, however, is presently offered in a few functional fields. Additionally, Columbia's Graduate School of Business cooperates with the School of International Affairs in offering a joint three-year program leading to two master's degrees, the M.B.A. and the Master of International Affairs.

Students at Harvard may concentrate in international business during the second year by taking three courses (semester system) involving case analyses of environmental and managerial problems in the international sphere, a research report course (required of all second-year students) in international business, and one of several area study seminars in government-business relations. That the international business courses at Harvard are grouped together rather than dispersed throughout the curriculum (either as separate courses or merged with existing courses) does not reflect the view that international business constitutes a separate "discipline" but instead that such an organization of courses represents the most efficient means of offering work in the field.

b. Several courses and no major. New York University (NYU) has a "combined" major, with the international work combined into the functional major. At NYU, students take noninternational courses in the functional field, international courses designed by functional faculty and offered through the functional department, and a few courses outside the functional area in international economics and international business itself. The center of gravity at NYU, therefore, is in the functional field, with complementary work offered in courses described as "international business." Environmental work in other departments (e.g., anthropology, political science) and theory courses in the department of economics may also be expected of students who elect the "combined."

The University of Wisconsin offered an M.B.A. with a "combined" major until the fall of 1966, when it established a major in international business. The University of Washington, which offers a major in international business, is tending in the direction of a "combined" major.

c. Minimal curriculum. Stanford University, Michigan State University, Northwestern University, and the University of Chicago are among the schools believing that students are best prepared for the challenges of international business by a strong background in the existing curriculum. Stanford, Michigan State, and Northwestern encourage their faculties to build into their courses the relevant international materials. At Chicago, students are introduced to the international dimension of business by formal study in two or three elective courses emphasizing international economics and finance, and for those who wish to put special emphasis on this area, by spending a year in work and study abroad. (Chicago's second-year program will be discussed under "Student Exchange Programs.") All four schools offer one or more courses in international economics; Stanford and Northwestern give an elective in the management of international enterprise; and Michigan State offers three electives in international business in the marketing department.

Teaching Aids

A potentially strong teaching aid is provided by the American Universities Field Staff (AUFS),[10] which is sponsored by 11 U. S. universities. Founded in 1951, AUFS is a nonprofit educational organization whose purpose is to disseminate in-depth knowledge about countries abroad for use by U. S. universities. Full-time AUFS personnel spend from one to three years in particular countries and return to give lectures on recent developments at the 11 sponsoring universities. Each year, from 60 to 100 reports, available by subscription from AUFS, are written on various problems by AUFS personnel.

An advanced simulation exercise in the form of a management game was developed several years ago at the University of Chicago. Known as the International Operations Simulation (INTOP), the game involves a corporation having a home office in Liechtenstein and subsidiaries in the United States, Brazil, and a European Economic Community (EEC) country. Players are presented with international challenges, and the game is designed to be used with lectures and discussions. It has been programmed for a variety of computers and has been used by many business schools (as well as some businesses) in the United States and abroad.[11]

Student Exchange

About 9.6 percent of all foreign students in U. S. higher educational institutions in 1965-66 were studying business administration. Of these 7,909 students, approximately 60 percent were enrolled at the undergraduate level. One-third of the students came from the Far East; 20 percent were from Latin America; North America (mainly Canada) supplied about 13 percent; Europe and the Middle East each provided about 11 percent; the African component was almost 8 percent.[12]

The most popular adjunct to international business curricula is the service offered by the Association Internationale des Etudiants en Sciences Economiques et Commerciales (AIESEC), based in Geneva. AIESEC arranges summer employment abroad for students from some 40 countries. All exchanges are reciprocal, so that a school sending a student to another country for summer work must arrange summer employment in its home country for a student from abroad. In 1966, AIESEC arranged for more than 4,500 business and economics students to go abroad, compared with 89 in 1949 and an expected 10,000 by 1970.[13] AIESEC-U. S.[14] has chapters (committees) at about 70 universities.

In addition to AIESEC, a few U. S. business schools offer student exchange programs in conjunction with schools abroad. Two of the most ambitious school-to-school exchange programs are given at the University of Oregon (for undergraduates) and the University of Chicago (for graduates). Since the 1965-66 school year, Oregon has operated a "junior year abroad" program specifically for students enrolled in the School of Business Administration. During the junior year, 20 to 30 students are exchanged between Oregon and The Netherlands Institute for Foreign Representation. They are accompanied by an exchange professor who teaches some of the courses to students from his home school during their stay abroad. Other courses in the exchange curriculum, including a foreign language that builds on sophomore work, are taught by resident faculty. Classes are conducted in English.

At Chicago, students may spend the second year of their M.B.A. program at either the London School of Economics and Political Science or the Université Catholique de Louvain, in Belgium. Students going to Louvain must be fluent in either French or Flemish. Chicago students are expected to take

16 of the normal 20 courses (quarter system) required for the M.B.A., omitting four electives. Hence, to complete the program in two years, they must attend the summer, fall, winter, and spring quarters of their first year on the Chicago campus. Some students, however, take the normal two years on the Chicago campus and go abroad in a third year. In the summer prior to their exchange year, they are employed in businesses abroad. The exchange coursework at each of the three schools is drawn from its regular curriculum and culminates in the granting of that school's regular degree. Thus, all students receive two degrees: the Chicago M.B.A. and either the Master of Science in Economics from London or the Licensié en Sciences Economiques Appliquées from Louvain. Eventually, the number of students participating in the program at any one time will be 10 to 20 from Chicago and 5 to 10 from each of the European schools. The overall Chicago program is shaped by the belief that international business is not a separate academic discipline and that students can best develop a sensitivity to the international environment by living, working and studying abroad.

Indiana University's business school, in a smaller program, exchanges two students each year with Catholic University, Paris.

At Massachusetts Institute of Technology, the MIT Fellows in Africa program, while not a two-way exchange, nonetheless provided MIT graduates with experience in government ministries, development corporations, and other agencies primarily concerned with industrial and economic development in several tropical African countries. Graduates went abroad for two years, thus combining experience overseas with technical assistance in developing countries. The last class of African Fellows was sent abroad in 1965. Since then, MIT has begun placing graduates in Colombian companies for two-year terms.

A collateral benefit of student exchange programs is the opportunity for faculty research resulting from the closer association of the participating schools.

Research

Less has been done to point the direction in research than in any other facet of education for international business. While some educators complain that not enough research has been done, others lament its mixed quality. An effective curriculum is founded on past achievements in research, and the lack of research is doubtless one of the principal causes of educators' wariness and uncertainty in fitting international business into the curriculum.

Examples of possible types of research in international business are: studies of domestic institutions and conditions in particular countries abroad or in groups of countries; comparative studies contrasting U. S. practices and institutions with those in one or more countries abroad; studies of special organizational and operational challenges that confront multinational corporations;

and studies of comparative environments, referring especially to political, social and cultural elements.

Of the research that has been done, the following suggest the range of research:

—the multinational organization and how it works (Harvard);

—capital budgeting and pricing in French nationalized industries (Berkeley);

—a summary and analysis of accounting practices in countries abroad (University of Washington and Chicago);

—industry's response to the emergence of the Central American common market (Wisconsin);

—comparative labor movements and collective bargaining (Cornell and Illinois), and comparative manpower policies (Berkeley, Michigan State and Chicago).

Research is expensive. Research in international business is particularly expensive. In the last two years, Ford Foundation grants have been used to establish research institutes at two midwestern universities: The Center for International Business Research, at Wisconsin, and the International Business Research Institute, at Indiana. Though only Wisconsin scholars have been given support in the Center's first year, the question of aid to applicants at other schools is still open. The aim of the Institute, which began in 1966, is to encourage team research. Both institutes plan to support the research of graduate students.

The University of Illinois has pioneered in international accounting by creating, in 1962, a Center for International Education and Research in Accounting. Through the auspices of the Center, numerous faculty from abroad (principally Europe and the Orient) have visited the school to teach and engage in research. The Center has published several research monographs, and in 1962 it held an International Conference on Accounting Education. In 1965, the Center inaugurated a semiannual journal devoted exclusively to international accounting.

A less technical and more managerially oriented periodical, the *Columbia Journal of World Business*, was introduced in 1965-66. A quarterly, it is published by the business school at Columbia University. Another quarterly journal, *The International Executive*, summarizes or annotates articles and books containing materials that are pertinent to the management of international operations.[15]

In 1959, several business school educators founded the Association for Education in International Business (AEIB). The organization currently has about 180 members, and serves as a clearinghouse for information on research projects and curricular developments. It meets annually in December, together with the American Economic Association and other social science associations.

Technical Assistance

Included under this heading are efforts to develop business schools and institutes abroad and to give instruction to students, educators, and business-men from other countries.

Since the mid-1950s, a number of U. S. business schools, encouraged by grants from the Ford Foundation, Agency for International Development (AID), and certain governments, have participated in technical assistance programs abroad. Major programs of this kind are administered by Harvard, Columbia, Stanford, Indiana, Michigan State, Georgia Institute of Tech-nology, Cornell, Massachusetts Institute of Technology, Washington Uni-versity (St. Louis), and the Midwest Universities Consortium for International Activities (MUCIA), among others. Most of the programs provide for assist-ance in administering and staffing newly emerging business schools in estab-lished universities, typically in less well developed countries.[16] In at least two instances business schools were created apart from any existing university, and in a number of instances (mostly in Europe) institutes were developed exclusively for instruction in business. While it would be impractical to discuss all the completed and on-going programs, the following survey gives some idea of what is being done.[17]

By any standard, Harvard has been the most active in these programs. From 1954 to 1964, it supplied 12 advisors from its faculty to the Institute of Business Administration at the University of Istanbul, Turkey, and 17 mem-bers of the Institute's faculty studied at the Harvard Business School. Since 1962, Harvard has been assisting in the development of the Indian Institute of Management, at Ahmedabad, as a result of which a number of executive training programs staffed by faculty from Harvard and the Institute have been offered in different Indian cities. Harvard has also been assisting in the creation of a Central American Institute of Business Administration (INCAE), which will be dedicated to teaching, research, and consultation in the field of management.[18] The Harvard faculty has also participated in executive training programs in several locations in the Central American isthmus. The most recent Harvard project is the development of a graduate business school in the Philippines in conjunction with three existing Philippine universities.

Through its International Teachers Program, begun in 1958, the Harvard Business School offers university or management institute teachers from abroad the opportunity to study on its campus. This program is currently being used to train teachers who will staff the INCAE school.

As an integral part of all its projects, Harvard collects case materials for use in its technical assistance programs, by students in the M.B.A. program at Harvard, and by educators generally. With support from the Ford Foundation, Harvard published a volume of citations to cases relevant to "multinational business,"[19] and is now in the process of compiling and referencing case materials for use in teaching business administration in different regions of the world. A volume of annotated case listings covering Latin America was the first one published.[20]

For a period of ten years—from 1954 to 1964—Michigan State University assisted in developing a business school in São Paulo, independent of any existing educational institutions in Brazil. In the view of one observer, the Escola de Administração de Emprêsas de São Paulo de Fundação Getulio Vargas is

> one of the strongest business education centers to be found in the developing countries. In the twelve years since its founding, it has developed undergraduate and graduate programs, a series of post-experience courses for practicing businessmen, a modest but relevant research program, full accreditation at the university level by the Ministry of Education, a faculty of nearly forty professors who have graduate degrees—and a new eight-story building.[21]

Although the privately run Getulio Vargas Foundation, the Ford Foundation, and AID in conjunction with Michigan State University played important roles, the major influence was the support provided by the community.

> In a pattern that is observable wherever management subjects are taught, businessmen contributed time and money to assist the new institution—and, equally important, they produced both the students and the jobs afterwards. This practical endorsement generated a level of business-academic contact that surely stimulated the sense of involvement and institutional growth of the São Paulo School.[22]

In 1962, Stanford established The International Center for the Advancement of Management Education (ICAME) under a Ford Foundation grant, for the purpose of giving courses in business to instructors from developing countries. The program is more structured than Harvard's International Teachers Program, as it offers an eight-month program designed specifically for the needs of the invited instructors from abroad.

Stanford also has directed the development of a graduate-level business school in Latin America, the Escuela de Administración de Negocios para Graduados (ESAN) in Lima, Peru. Partly because of the interdepartmental problems sometimes encountered when developing business schools in established universities abroad, ESAN was created apart from any existing university. The program was begun as part of the Alliance for Progress and has been financed by both the Peruvian and the United States governments. The Stanford curriculum was used as the model for the new school. One or two Stanford faculty members have been at the new school continually since its inception to guide its development. In addition to developing the new school, Stanford faculty members have conducted four-week executive development programs in Peru for Latin American business and government personnel.

Georgia Institute of Technology has had the principal role in assisting in the development of two 18-month executive programs at the Universidad del Valle, in Cali, Colombia. These programs were conceived in the early 1960s by a group of young Cali businessmen who were bent on developing the human and economic potential of the Cauca Valley region and of Colombia generally. The strongly felt needs of the community coalesced with the environment and resources of a university to produce programs, first, for the business leaders of Cali, and second, for promising young executives.[23] The first was intended to create the climate for the second. In part, the programs are structured around special projects in the participants' companies. A resident faculty, educated in the U. S. business schools, has been complemented by visitors from such schools as Stanford, Chicago and MIT.

Columbia University has played major roles in Turkey and Argentina. It has sent faculty members and doctoral candidates to Robert College, Istanbul, to offer courses and assist the resident staff in strengthening the school. In addition to offering lectures at the University of Buenos Aires, the Columbia faculty has for the last six years invited Argentine students to its M.B.A. and Ph.D. programs. More than 30 students, mostly on AID fellowships, have been admitted during the period.[24]

The Midwest Universities Consortium for International Activities—whose members are Wisconsin, Michigan State, Indiana and Illinois—recently began a cooperative technical assistance project with the Thai government in Bangkok. The four midwestern institutions, each of which is active overseas on its own, are helping to develop a new National Institute of Development Administration (NIDA), an institution blending work in business administration with studies in public administration, economics and statistics. The concept of NIDA is unique and is beamed directly at meeting the administrative needs of a developing country in both the private and public sectors.

Washington University (St. Louis) has shown that a medium-sized business faculty (about 30) can administer and staff technical assistance programs abroad. Between 1958 and 1964, under a series of AID contracts, the business school sent as many as five faculty members to Korea, where they conducted management development programs and assisted in the strengthening of business programs at Yonsei University and Korea University. The Washington faculty members, who were complemented by two men from other U. S. business schools, resided abroad for up to two years at a time. Since termination of the active phase, Washington faculty members, in cooperation with the AID mission, have spent summers in Korea to consult with the two schools. Washington also has invited 42 Tunisian students to enroll for three years in its undergraduate business program. Seventy percent of the students successfully completed their studies.

The large majority of technical assistance programs have been conducted abroad; of the total we have mentioned only a few of the programs that have involved U. S. business schools. In addition to examples already described, at least one other technical assistance program has been held in the United States, a four-week management course given by Tulane University in 1960 and 1962 for businessmen from Mexico and Costa Rica. AID provided the financial support.

Continuing Education

In addition to developing programs for businessmen from other countries, U. S. business schools have engaged in continuing education programs with international emphases for U. S. businessmen. Already mentioned were the executive programs offered abroad by faculty members from Harvard (India and Central America), MIT (India), Stanford (Latin America), Washington, St. Louis (Korea), and the Tulane program, which was held in the United States.

Columbia University has developed an Executive Program for International Managers. Emphasizing the use of modern management techniques in the context of political, economic and social conditions abroad, the four-week Columbia program has been given since 1960.

In 1965, Northwestern University developed a two-week program for senior executives and officers of multinational corporations. It is given once each year in Zurich.

Though not connected with a business school, the program offered at American University is of interest. It is administered by the School of International Service, and is designed to prepare executives and their wives for initial assignments abroad through emphasis on the social and cultural differences from the United States. Courses are offered in language, history, anthropology and related subjects. The program is sponsored by the Business Council for International Understanding of New York City.[25]

The programs outlined in this section are illustrative of the range of activities within reach of many business schools.

We will now attempt to explain the diversity of international business curricula among different schools, and then proceed to discuss the points to be considered by a school when designing its own strategy.

Conceptual Aspects of Making the Choice

EXPLANATION OF DIVERSE CURRICULA

The recitation of international business curricula as a sample of U. S. business schools, presented in the preceding section, attests more to diversity than sameness. This diversity may be explained in part by the different objectives and conditions at each school and in part by unresolved controversy that permeates faculty discussions of international business curricula. While we do not deny that a particular school's position in this controversy depends on the unique features of that school, the controversy itself brings to the surface a few unanswered questions that deeply concern educators in planning curricula in international business. An explanation of the controversy follows, together with a few comments on how it has evolved.

The controversy, in its earliest form, was whether international business deserved a niche somewhere in the business school curriculum. Prior to the 1950s, the answer at many schools was "yes" only to the extent of one or two courses in import-export management, usually offered through the marketing department. In addition, a course in international economics may have been offered, but typically only in the department of economics. During the 1950s, however, the dramatic developments in the overseas operations of U. S. businesses caused schools to reconsider the role of international business. Some rejected it out of hand, while others initiated cautious programs. As the number and variety of curricula in international business enlarged in the late 1950s and early 1960s, the controversy shifted from "yes" or "no" to "how should it be fitted into the curriculum?"

Now the controversy is at two levels: conceptual and pragmatic. At the conceptual level, the split is between those who believe international business represents an extension, or difference in degree, from the existing business curriculum, and those who contend that international business constitutes a separate and distinct field of study in certain of its aspects, while drawing on the existing curriculum for some support. The first position seems to imply that the existing curriculum should become internationalized by building into each course the relevant international aspects. In addition, a few courses in international business, perhaps "area study courses" (i.e., dealing with the business and economic conditions of specific geographic areas) or comparative courses, would be offered by the business school faculty with the possible assistance of faculty in other disciplines. Students might also be advised or required to take one or more existing courses in other departments for the cultural, political and social dimensions.

The second position favors a concentration or major in international business, with several course offerings in international business in addition to the existing curriculum. Students would also be encouraged to take environmental work in other departments.

At the pragmatic level, those who argue on conceptual grounds that the bulk of international business should be taught as part of existing courses concede unhappily that faculty members cannot—and in some instances will not—meet the challenge of acquiring competence in the international dimension of their fields. Successful integration, they believe, is many years off—

and it may be a dream. Today, it is necessary to support the existing curriculum with special courses in international business. Adherents to this view, however, do not agree on the shape of the resulting curriculum. Some (such as Harvard and Columbia) have chosen to group "international" courses together, permitting a concentration. For the time being, they believe, this is the expeditious approach. Others (including New York University) believe that while a few special international courses should be grouped apart from the existing curriculum, other courses should be developed in each of the existing functional areas (e.g., finance, marketing, accounting), and these functional areas, abetted by the new international courses designed by men in the functional fields, should be the only majors or fields of concentration. The burden of internationalizing the entire existing curriculum is therefore removed from the whole faculty and is assigned instead to one or two men in each functional field.

Other more cautious schools believe that a conceptual foundation must be laid prior to building a distinctive body of knowledge such as international business. In the meantime, they argue, essentially the same curriculum should be offered to all students with perhaps an elective course or two in international business.

The manner in which this controversy has evolved *partly* explains the configurations of a number of seemingly unrelated curriculum efforts at different schools. But it cannot be safely inferred from the nature of a curriculum that the faculty subscribes to one or another of the positions at either the conceptual or pragmatic levels of the current controversy. A host of other, less well-articulated considerations have acted to point curricula in still different directions. A potent factor is certainly the character of the core program required of all students, together with the degree of specialization allowed in functional fields. Another is the tractability of the faculty who might be asked to become involved in the international work. At a single school, moreover, the curriculum answer for international business may be different for graduates than undergraduates.

A PROPOSED CONCEPTUAL FRAMEWORK

The subjective aspect of education for international business, i.e., the determination of what business schools *ought* to be doing, all too frequently has been buried in discussions of what business schools *can* do. Ideally, these concerns should be resolved independently.

We offer the following analysis:

Whereas economic theory, statistics, and operations research are the same everywhere, the application of these disciplines to the solution of particular problems of policy must take into account differences in institutions, conventions, and business practices among different countries. Furthermore, large differences exist between the United States and other countries in such concerns of business as labor market practices, accounting practices, industrial organization, capital market structures and government-business relations. An understanding of these differences is of great importance to the international businessman even though it is impossible to point to—much less teach—a cohesive and integrated body of knowledge called "international business."

In time—perhaps over the next ten years—some structure may be developed in the field. *The extent to which some formal structure can be developed will depend in large part on the scope and perception of comparative research studies now under way and to be undertaken in the future.* Comparative studies in accounting, labor market practices, banking, advertising, and numerous other aspects of business operations will help to separate out those features which are really common to all or most countries, and thereby help to delineate the nature and contours of the institutional overlay which contains the truly international elements in business. Until we have much more of this kind of knowledge, any program of education in international business necessarily must be exploratory and experimental. Above all, it should be flexible.

Comparative research in virtually all the subject areas studied in business schools can provide insights not only into the problems of adapting to conditions abroad, but also into the assumptions and conditions taken for granted in the United States. In industrial relations, for example, comparative studies of diverse international labor market policies and practices, together with variegated collective bargaining patterns—all viewed in the context of the evolving social, economic, legal, and political conditions of each country—can prepare businessmen for the difficult process of understanding and accommodating to the unfamiliar environments abroad. Furthermore, such studies place in sharper relief the environmental factors that have shaped labor relations policies and practices in the United States. Similarly, in the field of finance, careful analysis of the factors influencing the configuration of financial arrangements in other countries provides perspective for understanding the variations in U. S. capital markets. We do not mean merely an enumeration of various financial institutions in countries X, Y and Z, but a deeper look at how these institutions came to be, how they serve the particular environment in which they exist, and how they are likely to interact with U. S. companies operating abroad.

In developing its approach to international business, each school faces three crucial questions:

1. *how best to mount a broad attack on international business problems;*
2. *how to design the curriculum;*

3. how to relate the entire program to the existing educational efforts of the school.

We start with the basic premise that any program must have a broad research base, for two reasons: (a) no teaching program at the graduate or professional level can be first-rate unless it is nourished and reshaped continuously by a flow of new knowledge, and (b) the vague and diverse field loosely called "international business" demands a broad and steady research effort in order to give it form and substance.

We have concluded that there is not now a formal body of knowledge, outside of international economics, sufficient to justify a host of special courses with "international" used mainly as an adjective. In addition, in matters of institutional differences and cultural understanding, a school in the United States can provide only a very pale substitute for work and study in an international environment. Following the principle of comparative advantage, we have decided that the important overlay of specialized institutional knowledge can best be provided by universities abroad, and that the U. S. business school could best prepare students in basic disciplines that would allow them to make most effective use of time spent abroad.

In order to preserve the integrity of a school's present—though changing—M.B.A. program, the rigor and content should not be watered down by an infusion of an excessive number of "international" courses at the expense of thorough education in the more basic disciplines and specialized courses in the functional fields. It is felt, in other words, that training in international business should in large measure supplement, and not replace, good fundamental study in business.

Strategies for Involvement

In the first section of this survey we explained why many business deans and faculties have been cautious in approaching the decision to become involved in international business programs. We proceeded to discuss recent developments in business education, relating them to the international business decision.

In the second section, we described a cross section of programs that business schools have offered or are offering. The survey disclosed that schools have selected many different mixes, or strategies, of educational activities.

In the third section, we offered an explanation for the diverse patterns of curricula found in the second section, and proposed a conceptual framework for thinking about a school's involvement in international business.

It is the purpose of the following section to discuss two broad determinants of strategy, including an enumeration of activities which schools should consider, and to discuss four classes of strategies covering different levels of involvement.

DETERMINANTS OF STRATEGY

1. Personalities of the university and the business school. Throughout this report, we have eschewed the idea of one solution for all schools. Each school and its university has its own capabilities and aspirations. These unique attributes must be assessed prior to determining a school's degree of involvement in international business.

First the university. What are some of these attributes?

Location and objectives. Universities situated in port cities or in large industrial cities may sense the need for a stronger international commitment because their communities are more internationally minded. Universities located at a distance from industries or ports, on the other hand, may feel an obligation to prepare their communities for the future challenges of international commerce—a developmental role. Inevitably involved in such determinations is whether the university views its sphere as international, national, regional or local. This judgment will profoundly affect the university's willingness to become committed to overseas operations or even to a curriculum with international pretensions.

Size and type of institution. Whether the university has a student body of 25,000 (probably including many students from abroad) or 5,000; whether it is a private or public institution—and, if the latter, whether it is in a coastal or inland state—these factors, too, have a bearing. Is the university growing in size and scope of activities, and would an international business dimension contribute to this growth?

Resources. Aside from the question of its *total* resources, the university must ask whether it has the *available* resources to support a strong international program. Has it had experience in securing and administering foundation and government grants?[26]

Next, the business school.

Depth of faculty interest. Is there a general interest, if not enthusiasm, among the school's faculty for international involvement? Schools that have had experience with international programs have reached near-unanimous agreement that such programs must touch the interests of more than a few faculty. Does the faculty interest appear to be genuine and long-term or does it seem to feed on the desire to emulate the current efforts of University X?

Relations with business community. Does the school have reasonably close relations with a business community that might provide encouragement and even support through financial grants, consultative engagements, or employment abroad for international faculty?

Depth of dean's interest. If the impetus for international business originates within the faculty, would the school's administration be enthusiastic, indifferent or skeptical? If the last two, the momentum and continual administrative support that an international program must have probably cannot be achieved.

Size and resources. Does the faculty possess the size and versatility to staff programs at home and abroad concurrently? Can the school afford to release faculty for one or two years of self-education prior to establishment of an international program? The school should also consider its ability to support research grants needed to complement a curriculum.

Relations with other departments. Will the school, especially its faculty, develop cooperative if not reciprocal relations with other university departments so that students of international business can easily enroll for work in such disciplines as economics, psychology, political science, language and anthropology? Indeed, are interdepartmental lines of communication truly open or is the university composed of intellectual islands? This departmental intercourse is crucial, for all but a very few business schools are unable to provide their own environmental coursework. Moreover, a continuing interdepartmental flow of ideas is likely to assist business school faculty in acquiring an understanding of different economies, political systems and cultures.

Support by university administration. Programs in international business can be expected to have hidden costs that appear unexpectedly at the most awkward times. Therefore, the ultimate question from a practical standpoint becomes: would an international program have the full support of the university administration? If not, the business school may not be able to extricate itself from embarrassing financial difficulties in the uncertain future.

These, then, are some of the critical questions that a business school must ask about its university and itself. Introspection and self-evaluation must precede any decision to embark on international paths.

2. Activities constituting a program in international business. A program for education in international business may consist of a combination of diverse activities, including curricula, technical assistance projects, faculty research, library enrichment, and continuing education programs. A preliminary step to developing the optimum combination for a particular school is an enumeration of the activities that might be considered. We present such a list which, if it is not exhaustive, is a rather large sample of what might be done. The list is graded from those activities requiring the least commitment of faculty and financial resources to those that demand heavy commitments.

A. The following activities require only a minimum commitment of resources.

1. Admit qualified students from abroad.
2. Start an AIESEC chapter.
3. Attempt to place students in summer employment abroad.

4. Invite special one- or two-day lecturers from government, multinational corporations, U. S. schools having strong international programs, and schools or companies abroad (if the individuals happen to be temporarily stationed or traveling in the United States).

5. Participate in interdepartmental international programs administered elsewhere in the university, perhaps offering one or two business courses modified somewhat by the international dimension.

6. Add or strengthen courses in international economics or international trade—the courses that in many universities are offered in the department of economics.

7. Invite local businessmen or government employees who occupy positions of responsibility in international operations to become businessmen-in-residence for the purpose of counseling faculty members and perhaps offering a course in international problems.

8. Invite teachers from abroad to take work in the school. Limit administration of the program to advising visitors on which course to take and to informal consultations with faculty. Offer no new courses. (Harvard offers an International Teachers Program in which seminars on curriculum building, research methods, and pedagogical techniques are especially added for the visitors. The addition of these seminars, as well as any other special work, would naturally enlarge the commitment over what is suggested in No. 8.)

9. Encourage a few faculty members to become educated in the international facets of their fields of study in order to introduce and integrate such materials into some of their courses.

B. The following activities require a larger commitment of resources to the international effort.

10. Initiate a student exchange program with a school abroad. No new courses need be developed, but at least one faculty member will need to devote considerable time, at least in the early years, to its administration.

11. Invite a visiting faculty member from abroad or from a U. S. school having a strong international program. Faculty contacts with the visitor might lead to further faculty willingness to develop international interests.

12. Ask faculty members generally to introduce and integrate international materials into existing courses.

13. Encourage students and faculty with international interests to develop or maintain competence in one or more of the major foreign languages.

14. Develop several new courses in international business, but do not create a major or concentration. While all faculty members should be interested, only a few will be actively involved. They may need leaves of absence and faculty research grants to prepare.
15. Add to library holdings in distinctively international materials. Naturally, the commitment for this activity can be large or small, but we feel that, to be of any value, the minimal acceptable effort is quite substantial.
16. Agree to support faculty research in international business, not only for those teaching international business, but for others.

C. The following activities require even larger commitments of resources, though in a few instances, *marked by an asterisk*, foundation or government grants are typically sought before schools become thus involved.

17. Hold a workshop or conference on recent developments in one or more aspects of international business, e.g., area studies.*
18. Conduct programs on the campus for businessmen from abroad.*
19. Arrange for faculty members to be employed in the overseas offices of multinational corporations or in the offices of companies abroad.
20. Allow faculty to participate in technical assistance programs administered by other universities.
21. Participate in continuing education programs administered by specific businesses for their employees. (While the *direct* costs of this activity may not be large, it presupposes the presence of at least a few faculty who have some international competence.)
22. Develop periodic programs in specific subject areas for the business community.
23. Gather comparative materials, e.g., cases. This activity, which will require travel abroad, can be integrated with participation in technical assistance programs and other faculty trips abroad. Hence, it may not be practicable as a *separate* activity.
24. Develop an international business curriculum sufficient to justify a major or concentration, but expect students to rely nonetheless on offerings in other departments. This activity may require rather extensive preparation abroad by several faculty members. Inclusion of this activity in the list does not imply that a major or concentration is a *normal* activity at this level of commitment, but only that the establishment of a major or concentration, if a school desires it, requires this level of commitment.
25. Participate in a technical assistance consortium with schools at several other universities. Administration of projects will be shared.

26. Recruit faculty who already have strong international backgrounds.
27. Develop consultative ties with business. This activity presupposes strong international competence among at least a few faculty members.
28. Conduct continuing education programs for businesses generally.

D. The following activities require a major commitment of resources, though in most instances, *marked by an asterisk,* foundation or government grants are typically sought before schools become thus involved.

29. Accept a technical assistance contract with a school abroad, but arrange to do most of the work in the U. S. After sending consultants and a few short-term lecturers to the school abroad, the U. S. school should invite students and faculty to come to the U. S. and study on its campus. The U. S. school should already be offering several international business courses (or have achieved successful integration of international materials in the existing curriculum) and should have strong relations with other departments in the university and with the business community.* (Example: Columbia.)
30. Develop a structured program with separate faculty to educate invited teachers from abroad.* (Example: ICAME, at Stanford.)
31. Adopt a permissive attitude toward faculty leaves for work or study abroad. This can be an expensive activity, especially when faculty research grants are awarded.
32. Inaugurate an international research center or institute.* (Examples: Wisconsin and Indiana.)
33. Start a journal devoted to international business. (Example: *Columbia Journal of World Business,* at Columbia.)
34. Accept technical assistance contracts with schools abroad, agreeing to perform most or all of the work abroad. This activity is open-ended, for such projects may be arranged with one school abroad or with several schools in different countries. Furthermore, faculty members may be required to remain abroad for from one to three years.*

We believe that this list is sufficiently representative to suggest the extent of commitment that schools should expect when contemplating different involvements. Many of the activities may be undertaken at any one of several scales of commitment. Moreover, some activities (e.g., a journal, curricula, exchange programs) ordinarily involve continuing commitments, while others (e.g., a visiting professor, a workshop) are one- or two-shot activities. Without question, the scale of commitment is more frequently underestimated in technical assistance programs abroad than in any other activity.

With these cautions in mind let us examine classes of strategies involving different levels of commitment.

3. Classes of strategies. We recommend that every school adopt a strategy. It should be a consciously developed strategy, not one followed as a result of indecision and procrastination.

Four classes of strategies are suggested for consideration by business schools. They may be divided into threshold strategies, lower-intermediate strategies, upper-intermediate strategies, and grand strategies.

Threshold strategies. Regardless of its resources, every school should accept a threshold involvement. At this level, costs are low and activities are easily undertaken. The opportunity cost of *not* doing so is high.

Activities 1 through 9 in the list presented earlier in this section fall within the threshold range. Essentially, these activities place reliance on the services or knowledge of persons outside the school, thus supplementing the existing curriculum with international aspects. AIESEC allows students to gain first-hand insights into different environments and institutions, while the presence of students and teachers from abroad (activities 1 and 8) introduce an international perspective into class discussions. Lecturers from business, government, and other schools can also establish the international link.

Schools that decide on a threshold strategy will develop only an ephemeral competence. They will be able to play support roles but will not be competent to participate on a continuing basis in frontier research and curriculum development. This role would fit most closely those schools with local or regional spheres of interest, and which do not have the resources to lead in international developments.

Lower-intermediate strategies. While activities in the threshold range provide an *exposure* to the international dimension, one that must be continually renewed because of the dependence on persons outside the school, lower-intermediate strategies are designed to provide a *base* upon which a school can build for the realization of possible long-term benefits. Activities 1 through 16, with at least some choices from those numbered 10 to 16, constitute the lower-intermediate range.

At this level, the establishment of a student exchange program or the development of a curriculum with international content are sources of new strength. Especially in developing a curriculum, the advice of a visiting faculty member who has a strong international background can be of great value. The critical ingredient, however, is faculty involvement in research, shown in the list as activity 16.

While the opportunities for real strides at this level are good, schools should not underestimate the costs. The ease with which student exchange programs are begun and administered should not be misjudged. They can require the full time of one or two faculty members, depending on the complexity of the plan.

One possibility, not yet tried, is an exchange program between a group of U. S. schools and a group of schools abroad. Shared administration and the exchange of ideas that is facilitated by formal relations among universities *on the business school level* are obvious benefits. This quasi-consortium could be easily expanded to include the cross-registration of students among the U. S. schools and perhaps even mutual visitations of faculty. Cooperative arrangements among U. S. universities, not only in activities performed abroad but also in curricula at home, will increasingly be the best means of undertaking expensive programs.

Consequently, one possible lower-intermediate strategy would involve an AIESEC chapter, an exchange program with one of the increasing number of business schools abroad, a few faculty research grants involving travel abroad, and the development of one or two courses in international business with the eventual aim of integrating the international work into existing courses. All of these activities cannot feasibly be begun at the outset. A reasonable progression is indicated by the order in which they are shown in the penultimate sentence, above. The creation of a major or concentration in international business depends on the availability and strength of other disciplines, the research, work experience, and depth of international interest in the business school faculty, and the ability and willingness of the school's administration to provide continuing financial and moral support. Concentrations in international business, no less than those in other fields, should not be undertaken lightly. They are therefore reserved for upper-intermediate strategies.

Upper-intermediate strategies. As the international involvement of faculty grows into the upper-intermediate range, i.e., including the activities numbered 17 through 28, the school is prepared to make important contributions. At this level, faculty members will engage in many more ventures to enhance their international competence, including technical assistance programs, case-gathering missions, and individual or joint research projects of other kinds. But it is at this level, too, where schools sometimes trip and fall. They must be cautious not to minimize the cost both in terms of faculty and funds. The transition between lower-intermediate and upper-intermediate strategies is perhaps the hardest to make, and schools must prepare themselves for the considerably larger scale of operations. In this connection several points are worth making.

First, the international interests of faculty members must be carefully gauged prior to authorizing initial travel grants. The attractiveness of travel abroad can divert productive faculty into habitual nomads and picture-takers, who remember little of their work and much of their pleasures.

It is important to distinguish genuine emissaries from junketeers, but all applicants should be asked to prepare detailed plans of accomplishment in terms of curriculum and research.

Second—and tied to the first point—is the relation of faculty research and travel to curriculum development. One of the most important returns from the investment of faculty time in research and technical assistance programs is *feedback* for curriculum improvement. A faculty member at one of the schools most active in technical assistance indicated that his school's biggest problem was lack of feedback by returning faculty. The inability or unwilling-ness of faculty to make the connection between truly international experiences and the coursework back home underscores the difficulty of persuading faculty to integrate international materials into existing courses. One barrier, cer-tainly, is that U. S. textbooks are weak on international dimensions. Knowing this, faculty should endeavor to create their own teaching materials—cases and lecture notes on environments and institutions are examples. Another barrier is that faculty members sometimes go abroad in a field other than their own. In the absence of unusual circumstances, it is wasteful for faculty spe-cializing in one field to go abroad in order to do work in another, simply to fill a need in the other country. As in other school efforts, each activity in international business should be programmed to contribute the optimum amount to the total school effort. Unrelated or disengaged activities are inefficient.

Third, care must be taken not to overestimate what can be accomplished in activities abroad, because unfamiliar customs and the usual absence of col-lateral facilities (e.g., technical libraries, rapid and frequent air and rail transportation, computers and machines for duplicating manuscripts, air con-ditioning) may delay the completion of projects to the point that they cannot be finished at all. Once abroad, the teacher-researcher finds that novel and intriguing situations, ripe for case writing and other types of research, are all around. In gathering data, he should be careful to make explicit the dis-tinctive features of the environment.

The upper-intermediate level offers exciting opportunities for growth, though such growth must be carefully watched if the school wishes to avoid drifting into the grand strategy range. Projects begin to multiply. One day the school may discover that, with one faculty member helping University X with its AID contract, a second on a consultation tour with Y Corporation in India, a third on a lecture in Europe, a fourth on research leave in South America, and a fifth on leave as an employee in the Istanbul office of Z Cor-poration, its policy on faculty leaves has been decreed by the growth in its international business program. As word spreads that a business school has some eager faculty with strong backgrounds in the international aspects of one or more functional fields, opportunities will create themselves. Schools must attempt to temper this growth (without despiriting the faculty) until they can afford to release the faculty from teaching duties for periods of a semester or a year. A price of growth is further growth.

Grand strategies. The grand strategy, including activities 29 through 34, should be considered only by the most affluent schools. The converse of this statement should be a guide to foundations and governments: grand programs should seek out only the affluent schools. If only because a school's span of attention and span of control have finite limits that are not known until they are exceeded, more difficulties have arisen out of participation in programs abroad than in any other activity.

If a school is to become engaged in an institution-building effort abroad, it should do so gradually, and only after full exploration and inquiry at home and abroad. The body of experience with overseas programs is now rather large, and, as far as possible, past errors should be avoided. The list of suggestions and warnings is large:

a. Do not underestimate the need for a broad and serious commitment by the school and university if the job is to be well done. The time and financial costs are high. Furthermore, programs abroad may lead to unforeseen commitments after the initial enthusiasm and newness of the enterprise have worn off.

b. From the outset, as the program is being negotiated, plan and build in as much research and graduate student participation as possible. A project which is entirely structured to serve only teaching needs abroad will inevitably prove less satisfying to good faculty members and diminish the potential "feedback" to knowledge and activity at home.

c. The U. S. business school should fit service abroad by faculty members into its system of rewards. Promotions and salary increases should not be denied to faculty members who have performed effectively abroad, although it should be made clear that these efforts should eventually be integrated with teaching and research activities at the home school.

d. Determine carefully that persons sent abroad have the personal adaptability and the professional qualifications for successful completion of the assignment. In some instances, programs abroad have suffered because of unwise staffing.

e. For assignments undertaken with foundation or government support, consider in advance whether, upon expiration of the grant, the program will be concluded or whether the school will make arrangements for its continuation. Institution-building strategy should take into account the long-range possibilities.

f. A few of many possible practical suggestions are:
   i. Be sure that at least one person who can speak and write the local language is present at all times. Interpreters, especially simultaneous interpreters, are not always available.
   ii. Prior to leaving, investigate the problems of dealing with the government abroad. Inquiries may be made through the De-

partment of State or other universities that have been active in the particular country.

iii. Prior to leaving, apply to the home office of companies for letters of introduction to overseas offices. Do not underestimate the difficulty of obtaining cooperation from businesses abroad and the overseas offices of U. S. companies.

iv. When involved in short-period teaching activities abroad, especially in executive programs, take time to learn the special conditions and problems that confront businessmen in the host country. This effort may require one or two months of consultation with businessmen in that country.

Grand strategies, if executed with sufficient resources and effective long-term planning, can contribute significantly to the accumulation of knowledge on the uncertain subject of international business. It is at this level, as well as the upper-intermediate level, that valuable comparative studies can be undertaken. Moreover, because of their participation in programs being administered by schools at the grand-strategy level, other schools, less well endowed, will depend on the bigger schools for their own development.

Innumerable variations of these strategies may be devised by combining different activities and varying the scale on which each is undertaken. Schools able to undertake a grand strategy, and schools at which the threshold strategy is appropriate, are easier to identify than are the many schools that might fall within the large intermediate-strategy range. The best general counsel in such cases is to begin in the threshold-strategy range and gradually increase the degree of commitment in the light of continual reevaluations of school capabilities and goals. While the counsel offered by schools having larger programs may be helpful at times, care should be taken to keep clearly in mind the different capabilities and goals of the two types of schools.

Implications for Foundations, Government and Business

It is clear that business schools can perform a multiplicity of roles in education for international business. Many schools currently feel pressured to *do something* in international business. The most visible activity consists of technical assistance programs abroad. But they are easy to turn on and hard to shut off. Schools must be encouraged gradually to develop competence in international business, and for most a beginning at the level of threshold strategy is most sensible.

Foundations and governments can contribute to this development in several ways. First, they should avoid dispersing funds for technical assistance programs too thinly. Based on a knowledge of the aspirations and resources of each school and university, foundations and governments should identify schools that are capable of carrying out the designated activities. The grants might provide that other schools which have developed intermediate-level competence be invited to participate in staffing the programs abroad on a limited basis. In this manner, intermediate-level schools will have the opportunity to develop their talents at an even rate without being tempted to "rush for the gold" of their own programs abroad.

Second, foundations should encourage the cooperation of U. S. schools in expanding their activities into the intermediate level. The idea of a consortium to combine the area study strengths of groups of schools would discourage each from attempting to become proficient in a full range of programs—an objective that has eluded even the most affluent schools.

Third, foundations should encourage the creation of research institutes through which other schools as well as the home school can carry out research activities. Research in international business can be an expensive activity at business schools, because to a greater extent than with research in other fields, faculty members must be on leave for considerable periods of time. The school's need to replace the teaching vacancy with a visitor would mean, if the school is supporting the faculty member's research, that the total cost is quite large. The existence of several research institutes which would encourage projects undertaken by faculties at other schools could alleviate this financial burden.

American business is attaching increasing importance to the international dimension in the training and background of the men who are selected for leadership positions.[27] Through a variety of activities, business schools are attempting to provide guidance to businesses in meeting the challenges of conducting international operations. Benefits will accrue to businesses through better educated graduates (both in the U. S. and abroad), research studies on international topics, continuing education programs, and consultative relationships with faculty members. In order to develop capabilities, the business schools need financial and moral support from the business community. This support can take the form of grants to selected universities, consultative opportunities, making research data available, or offers of employment in overseas offices. Whatever the nature of the link between business schools and the business community, it is of overriding importance that such a link exist.

Notes

[1] While master's and doctor's programs have grown in recent years, enrollment in undergraduate business programs has continued to increase apace. The Committee for Economic Development reports: "One out of five men enrolled in college is now majoring in business. From a few hundred students in the early years of this century, enrollment in collegiate schools of business climbed above 400,000 by 1960 and is expected to reach 600,000 by 1970. United States Office of Education figures show that the 47,600 degrees conferred in business and commerce in 1960, plus the 6,800 degrees in economics, exceed the collective number of degrees granted in the biological sciences, the physical sciences, English and journalism, foreign language and literature, philosophy, geography, sociology, history, and anthropology." *Educating Tomorrow's Managers*, New York: The Committee for Economic Development, 1964, p. 10.

[2] American Association of Collegiate Schools of Business, *Faculty Requirements and Faculty Supply in Collegiate Business Teaching, 1954-1970*, St. Louis, 1954.

From 1954 to 1964 the percentage of faculty with doctorates in schools belonging to the Association increased from 56 to 71. *The American Association of Collegiate Schools of Business, 1919-1966*, Homewood, Illinois: Richard D. Irvin, Inc., 1966, p. 25. For a discussion of some of the problems brought about by the rapid growth of these programs, see Robert D. Buzzell, "The New Challenge for Doctoral Programs in Business," *Harvard Business School Bulletin*, Vol. 41, November-December 1965, pp. 17-19.

[3] *Higher Education*, Report of the Committee appointed by the Prime Minister under the Chairmanship of Lord Robbins, 1961-63, London: Her Majesty's Stationery Office, 1963.

[4] *British Business Schools*, Report by Lord Franks, London: British Institute of Management, November 1963.

[5] This expansion is described in "Britain's Business Schools," *The Economist*, January 15, 1966, pp. 198-202.

[6] Neither of the two major 1959 studies of American higher education in business administration (Robert A. Gordon and James E. Howell, *Higher Education for Business*, New York: Columbia University Press, 1959; Frank C. Pierson, *The Education of American Businessmen*, New York: McGraw-Hill, 1959) devoted specific attention to the international aspects of curricula, except for the suggestion that some humanities and fine arts courses relating to a foreign culture would be desirable preparation in the light of the changing nature of the world in which business operates. Even in their chapter on doctoral programs, Gordon and Howell make no reference to international studies or research. The Master of Business Administration curriculum suggested by Pierson does not include international subject matter; nor do either of the two master's programs proposed in the Gordon-Howell report. The undergraduate curricula proposed in these two reports similarly make no reference to any international aspects. However, both propose substantial requirements for undergraduate work in the humanities and in behavioral and other social sciences which might supply a limited international background of a nonprofessional character.

[7] *Samples:* Business Law in International Operations, The Pacific Coast States and Canada in International Trade, Europe and the U.S.S.R. in World Business, Underdeveloped Areas in World Business (seminar). Seven of the courses are area studies and six deal with logistics.

[8] *Samples:* Legal Aspects of International Business and Investment, in the Department of Law; Comparative Industrial Relations, Comparative Social Insurance, in the Department of Economics and Finance.

[9] *Undergraduate samples:* Middle East and African Markets, Foreign Credit and Collection Management, Ocean Marine Insurance, Ocean Shipping, Interna-

tional Department Bank Operations, International Advertising. *Graduate Samples:* Analysis of International Transportation, Advanced Import Marketing, Tanker Management and Operation, Comparative Marketing Systems.

[10] The address of the American Universities Field Staff is 366 Madison Avenue, New York, N.Y. 10017.

[11] Hans B. Thorelli and Robert L. Graves, *International Operations Simulation,* New York: The Free Press of Glencoe, 1964; Hans B. Thorelli, Robert L. Graves, and Lloyd T. Howells, "The International Operations Simulation at the University of Chicago," *The Journal of Business,* Vol. 35, July 1962, pp. 287-297; and Hans B. Thorelli, "Simulating International Business Operations," in Stefan H. Robock and Lee C. Nehrt (eds.), *Education in International Business,* Proceedings of the International Business Administration Conference, Indiana University, December 1963, Bloomington: Graduate School of Business, Indiana University, 1964, pp. 56-67.

[12] Statistics on student and faculty exchange are taken from *Open Doors, 1966,* New York: Institute of International Education, pp. 11, 13, 15, 28-33.

In contrast to the interest shown by students, less than one percent of the foreign faculty members and scholars who came to U.S. educational institutions in 1965-66 were in business. This was the lowest percentage in that category of exchange.

Business administration was the major field of study for 3.6 percent of the U. S. students abroad in 1964-65, a higher percentage than the fields of engineering, education and agriculture, but much lower than the medical and social sciences, humanities, and the natural and physical sciences. Among the major academic and professional fields of American faculty members who worked overseas in 1965-66, business administration supplied the lowest percentage (2.8 percent).

The small numbers of foreign scholars coming to the United States and the small numbers of American students and faculty members in this field who go overseas for study or research may reflect the limited development of professional education in business administration in foreign countries.

[13] "The AIESEC Traineeship Exchange Programme," *The Quarterly Journal of AIESEC International,* Vol. 2, November 1966, p. 27.

[14] The address of AIESEC-U.S. is 51 East 42nd Street, New York, N.Y. 10017.

[15] The address of this journal, which is published privately, is: 64 Ferndale Drive, Hastings-on-Hudson, New York.

[16] The American Association of Collegiate Schools of Business has published a list of universities abroad that offer business programs, entitled *International Directory of Programs in Business and Commerce, 1966.*

In the spring of 1966, the American Association of Collegiate Schools of Business (AACSB) and the Overseas Educational Service (OES), an organization which recruits American educators to teach in colleges and universities in developing countries, compiled a roster of the international interests of the faculty members of the AACSB institutions. Both AACSB and OES have retained copies of the roster, which will be updated annually. Overseas Educational Service will utilize the information to contact particular individuals in instances where their qualifications match those needed in particular international programs.

[17] In a recent speech, "A Worldwide Campus for Management," Marshall A. Robinson surveyed some of the work being done under technical assistance programs. Reprints of the speech may be obtained from Office of Reports. The Ford Foundation, 477 Madison Avenue, New York, N.Y. 10022.

[18] For a report on progress during the first two years, see *The Harvard Business School—INCAE Project, 1963-65,* A Report of the Activities of the Harvard Graduate School of Business Administration in Central America, prepared by George C. Lodge, Director, Division of International Activities.

[19] Grace V. Lindfors (ed.), *Bibliography: Cases and Other Materials for the Teaching of Multinational Business,* Boston: Graduate School of Business Administration, Harvard University, 1964.

[20] Ruth C. Hetherston (ed.). *Bibliography: Cases and Other Materials for the Teaching of Business Administration in Developing Countries—Latin America,* Boston: Graduate School of Business Administration, Harvard University, 1966.

[21] Marshall A. Robinson, *op cit.,* p. 2.

[22] *Ibid.,* p. 3.

[23] For a report by one of the initiators, see Roderick F. O'Connor, "This Revolution Starts at the Top," *Columbia Journal of World Business,* Vol. 1, Fall 1966, pp. 39-46.

[24] A report on the program with the University of Buenos Aires is described in William L. Chapman, "Experiment in Argentina: The Bitter and the Sweet," *Columbia Journal of World Business,* Vol. 1, Fall 1966, pp. 49-56.

[25] A unique international program, designed to help prepare European and American business executives (and their wives) for working and living on each others' continents, is scheduled to open in February 1967 under the auspices of the Centre d'Echanges Technologiques Internationaux, at Cahors, France. The Graduate School of Public and International Affairs of the University of Pittsburgh is assisting in the development of the cross-cultural sensitivity aspects of the curriculum.

[26] For a perceptive analysis of the role of the university in technical assistance programs abroad, see the special study made for the Agency for International Development by John W. Gardner, then president of the Carnegie Corporation: *AID and the Universities,* New York: Education and World Affairs, 1964. On pages 22-23, Gardner recommends criteria that AID might use in selecting universities for its programs.

[27] A survey of the presidents and executives of the nation's 100 largest industrial firms found the following: "As another example of how routes to the top are determined by the over-all direction of the corporation, in our base period [1948-1953] almost none of the presidents had ever worked in the division or suborganization that handled foreign business. Because the large industrial corporation is going abroad more each year, more presidents are coming from the group dealing with foreign markets and manufacturing. By 1961-1965, 20 percent of the presidents had spent at least five years in staff or line assignments overseas. If the present trend continues, by 1970 the majority of our presidents will have had experience in managing foreign assignments at some time in their careers." Eugene E. Jennings, "You Can't Succeed in Business By Merely Trying," *Nation's Business,* Vol. 54, May 1966, pp. 115-116.

Selected Bibliography

(Compiled by Alice Tetelman, Research Assistant)

Advisory Committee on Private Enterprise in Foreign Aid. U. S. Agency for International Development. *Foreign Aid Through Private Initiative.* Report of the Committee, Arthur K. Watson, chairman. Washington, D.C.: Agency for International Development, July 1965.

Aitken, Thomas. *A Foreign Policy for American Business.* New York: Harper & Brothers, 1962.

Developing Management for the Worldwide Enterprise. A Business International Research Report. New York: Business International, 1965.

*Fayerweather, John, Jean Boddewyn and Holger Engberg. *International Business Education.* New York: Workshops in International Business, New York University, 1966.

Grégoire, Roger. *Business Management.* Paris: Unesco, The University Teaching of Social Sciences Series, 1966.

Lee, James A. "Cultural Analysis in Overseas Operations," *Harvard Business Review,* Vol. 44, March-April 1966, pp. 106-114.

Lindfors, Grace V. (ed.). *Bibliography: Cases and Other Materials for the Teaching of Multinational Business.* Boston: Graduate School of Business Administration, Harvard University, 1964.

Mace, Myles L. "The President and International Operations," *Harvard Business Review,* Vol. 44, November-December 1966, pp. 72-84.

Robinson, Marshall A. "A Worldwide Campus for Management." An address given at a meeting of the Association of Canadian Schools of Business, Sherbrooke, Quebec, June 6, 1966. Reprints available through the Office of Reports, The Ford Foundation, 477 Madison Avenue, New York, N.Y. 10022.

Robinson, Mary E. *Education for Social Change: Establishing Institutes of Public and Business Administration Abroad.* Washington, D.C.: The Brookings Institution, 1961.

*Robock, Stefan H. and Lee C. Nehrt (eds.). *Education in International Business.* Proceedings of the International Business Administration Conference, Indiana University, December 1963. Bloomington: Graduate School of Business, Indiana University, 1964.

Sinowitz, Barret N. "Promoting International Business as a Career," *The Quarterly Journal of AIESEC International,* Vol. 1, May/August 1965, pp. 11-13.

Thorelli, Hans B. and Robert L. Graves. *International Operations Simulation.* New York: The Free Press of Glencoe, 1964.

* Recommended for thoughtful discussion of strategies in curriculum design.

THE WORLD AFFAIRS ASPECTS
OF EDUCATION IN PUBLIC ADMINISTRATION

Why a World Affairs Interest?

The United States has belatedly begun to appreciate the complexity of the world setting to which it must respond politically, militarily, economically and ideologically. Only in the past decade have the implications and obligations of U. S. leadership begun to be understood. We have not yet adequately faced up to the policy and programmatic consequences of our international posture. Nor have we recognized that our responsibilities are of a long-run nature which will require this country, over the indefinite future, to devote a substantial part of its manpower and other resources to the search for world peace and progress.

These international concerns have a special significance for professional education in public administration. Governmental instrumentalities must bear the basic burden of planning and executing programs designed to deal with international problems. The world affairs aspects of governmental activity involve every major federal agency; they also draw upon the personnel resources of state and local government. The number of administrative, professional, and technical personnel needed to enable our public services to carry on their internationally related work not only will mount, but these individuals will require knowledge, sensitivity, and skill far more penetrating than our educational institutions have usually provided.

The schools of public administration must prepare increasing numbers of graduates for a variety of new, delicate and intricate international tasks. These include work in the agencies most directly concerned with U. S. foreign relations such as the State and Defense departments, the Agency for International Development, and the United States Information Agency. They also include positions in the many other federal departments and agencies which are involved in overseas economic and social development and other international activities. Personnel with state and local governmental experience are especially sought for assignments in the provision of technical assistance in public administration to newly emerging nations.

The mobility of U. S. governmental personnel among levels of government and among agencies means that many public administration graduates who start in essentially domestic governmental activities will move into internationally related positions at a later stage of their careers. A noteworthy recent development in several schools has been the provision of supplementary "capstone" training to individuals who are already qualified in a professional field, such as agriculture, engineering, education or health, but who wish additional preparation in generic public administration, in the administration of international activities, and in the practice of their profession in a foreign setting.

Intergovernmental agencies, such as those in the United Nations system, are seeking persons who have been trained to combine technical knowledge of administration with ability to function effectively in a multinational environment. International voluntary agencies are searching for individuals with similar qualifications.

U. S. schools of public administration also have an important role in the education of foreign students who are preparing themselves to improve governmental operations in their own countries. On a longer range basis, our schools have an even more significant function in their assistance in the development of indigenous public administration schools and institutes overseas.

But what of those U. S. administrators who—by choice or lack of opportunity—devote their careers to governmental functions which have little or no international content? Does professional education fulfill its obligation to this group of public administrators if it provides them with no significant insight into the practice of their profession outside the United States?

One of the classical elements of a profession is a systematic body of knowledge of substantial intellectual content; one of the inherent requirements of a professional practitioner is participation in the increase of this knowledge. While some aspects of public administration are more advanced in the United States than in other parts of the world, U. S. public administrators still can learn much from other countries' experience which will enhance their own competence. Many of our administrative doctrines and practices have their roots in the governmental systems of foreign nations. A true understanding of our own methods of organization and operation requires knowledge of the environments in which they had their origin. Moreover, even if their own official responsibilities do not involve any international content, U. S. administrators share a professional identity and a community of interest with fellow administrators in foreign nations who are doing work analogous to their own. Thus the very concept of a profession in public administration demands that Americans who consider themselves to be professional practitioners have a concern with the practice of their profession in other countries.

The Development of Professional Education in Public Administration

The history of U. S. professional education in public administration is a recent one. The antiquarian might discover a few pre-World War I beginnings. The New York Bureau of Municipal Research was founded in 1906 and the University of Michigan's Institute of Public Administration celebrated its 50th anniversary in 1965. But the broad stream of development dates from the mid-twenties, at the earliest. Syracuse University inherited the training branch of the New York Bureau of Municipal Research; the presently styled Maxwell School was established there in 1924. The University of Southern California started its school in 1928. Leonard D. White and W. F. Willoughby published the first textbooks of public administration in 1926 and 1927 respectively.

The study of public administration as an academic discipline originated in the departments of political science of the major universities. Despite the fact that most departments initially were apprehensive about its professional nature, what captured the interest of the academic founding fathers of the new study was the zeal of civic reform. Another point of origin for education in public administration was the research bureaus established by various state universities to help solve state and local governmental problems. These bureaus frequently undertook teaching, as well as research and community service functions.

The Present Status of Academic Organization

Several forms of organization for public administration education have developed: (a) a program or concentration within a political science or government department; (b) an autonomous curriculum or institute, related to such academic departments, but somewhat separate from them; (c) an independent professional school, sometimes combined with a professional school of business administration.[1]

The present trend is toward the independent professional school. There seems to be a growing tacit recognition of the need for *professional* teaching of public administration at the university level, but there is still resistance to frank acknowledgment of this status in many institutions.

The most recent comprehensive study of U. S. professional education in public administration was conducted by the Office of Education of the Department of Health, Education, and Welfare in 1960.[2] Its coverage was limited to graduate, degree-granting programs. In this category it identified 145 programs in 83 colleges and universities. The survey did not deal with specialized public administration programs at the undergraduate level.

The Council on Graduate Education in Public Administration, the national association of schools and programs in this field, collected data on graduate programs in 52 institutions for 1964-65 and 1965-66. Twenty-one of these programs were located within departments of political science or government and 16 were in autonomous curricula or institutes. Fifteen were separately organized graduate professional schools, five of which also offered programs in business administration.[3]

The educational influence of the graduate professional schools is far greater than these numbers would indicate. These schools enrolled more than 80 percent of the approximately 3,500 full-time and part-time graduate students in public administration. Ten of the 15 schools had full-time enrollments in excess of 40 students; the largest were Southern California (121), Pittsburgh (104), New York University (85), Syracuse (79) and Princeton (72). Southern California also had the largest group of part-time students (587), followed by Puerto Rico (177), State University of New York (144), City College of New York (136) and New York University (114).

The Council on Graduate Education in Public Administration is now engaged in an evaluative study of public administration education. This study will examine in detail the professional character of education in this field, especially as related to the professionalization of government as a field of practice.

Degrees and Professors

Most professional study in public administration is at the postgraduate level. There are a few undergraduate programs but they are essentially preprofessional rather than professional. They involve only a limited number of hours of special courses and usually represent a minor element in fulfilling the requirements for a liberal arts degree, with some emphasis upon social sciences.

By far the most common degree is the Master's, ordinarily the M.P.A. (Master of Public Administration). It is regarded as the terminal degree for the practitioner. A small number of institutions give a professional doctorate, usually the D.P.A. (Doctor of Public Administration). A larger number grant the Ph.D. as preparation for university teaching and advanced research in public administration.

Office of Education statistics[4] indicate that the number of Bachelor's and first professional degrees in public administration earned in U. S. higher educational institutions remained in the range of approximately 450 to 500 during the five academic years from 1959-60 through 1963-64. During the same five years, the number of Master's degrees increased from 158 to 400. The number of doctorates in public administration has been small, the greatest number reported being 29 in 1961-62 and again in 1962-63, with 23 such degrees in 1963-64. These figures probably are not complete, since some students who major in public administration receive degrees without any specialized designation.[5]

The professional schools are the principal sources of graduate degrees. The data collected by the Council on Graduate Education in Public Administration indicates that 76 percent of the graduate degrees are awarded by professional schools, 13 percent by programs in disciplinary departments, and 11 percent by autonomous curricula or institutes. Similarly, three quarters of the doctoral students are enrolled in separately organized professional schools.

A substantial proportion of graduate students in public administration do not complete their work for a degree. Experience of several schools indicates that many full-time students accept public service employment when they complete their formal course work, intending to finish the thesis or other academic requirements at a later time. Most of these apparently do not accomplish this objective. Part-time students are even less likely to fulfill the requirements for a degree. This apparently explains, in part at least, the discrepancy between the estimate of 2,300 to 2,500 graduate students working on Master's degrees in public administration in 1959-60 given by institutions participating in the 1960 survey,[6] and figures of 158 and 264 for earned Master's degrees awarded in 1959-60 and 1960-61 respectively.

While the number of doctoral candidates is increasing and the current doctoral programs are producing more graduates, they are insufficient to replace the present faculties of public administration, let alone to staff the expansion now taking place and contemplated for the future. This shortage is a grave one, even under the assumption that at least half of the public administration faculty will be recruited directly from other academic disciplines, such as political science, economics or sociology, or from other professional fields, such as engineering, business or law.

There is urgent need for additional financial resources to enable schools to expand their doctoral programs and support students preparing for teaching and research. The federal administration has recognized the importance of improving the caliber of public service at the national, state and local levels, and is preparing legislation on public personnel education and training for the 1967 Congress. Some financial assistance to the institutions which provide such education, together with aid for the students who receive it, is expected to be included in the legislative proposals.

Expansion to Meet the Future

Unfortunately, it is not enough to speak of replacing the present faculties of public administration in the United States. There is need for several times the sixty-odd programs and schools of public administration presently operating in the United States. And there is also need for the following: strengthening existing programs, not only to enable them to produce more practitioners, but also to increase the number of professors they prepare; for in-service as well as preservice education, including assisting government agencies with their own in-service training programs; and, most relevant, undertaking much more on the international front, in research as well as in education and training.

It is difficult to be precise as to the expansion required, but the schools still need to produce at least 5,000 persons with graduate degrees a year. This would involve a ten-fold increase over the present annual number. The demand for personnel with these qualifications comes not only from the federal government, but increasingly from state and local authorities, and from international agencies. The expansion of public services at the state and local level as part of the developing pattern of the "new federalism" intensifies the need for public administrators capable of dealing with complex administrative relationships, especially those involved in urban planning and urban administration, and for subject-matter specialists competent to organize and supervise large-scale operations.

The Generalist and the Curriculum

The special province of the public administration school is its general, unlimited concern for the entirety of the processes and policies of government and for their effective functioning. Public administration shares medicine's concern for public health, engineering's for public works, social work's for public welfare, law's for law enforcement and the courts. Public administration is involved in the activities of all professions, but it goes beyond their individual public service concerns to the total workings of government.

The essential focus of public administration is upon the process of formulating public policy, the expression of that policy in legislation and other vehicles, and the translation of policy into action through governmental instrumentalities. Within this broad area it is also concerned with the generic processes of management, with the techniques of planning, organizing and controlling governmental programs and with the effective energizing and coordination of all government operations.

The pioneers at curriculum building in public administration had more modest, immediate goals in mind. They sought to create a core of what might be termed "management generalists" who were management generalists because they were specialists in budgeting, personnel management and in organizing and coordination. The early graduates were to be specialists in technique, but they were to be generalists as to the subject-area. They presumably were to be competent to direct any type of public program. The important consideration was their ability to manage, since they were expected to absorb enough of the requisite substantive knowledge on the job to enable them to operate in any field.

Along with this early emphasis upon generalized management was the doctrine that administration and policy should be separated. This separation also was in line with the British system as it was then understood. The expansion of federal government activities and the development of strong executive leadership during the Roosevelt era brought new understanding of the relationships between administration and policy. At a later period, career administrators became inextricably involved in the goals of the New Frontier and of the Great Society. Parallel changes in outlook have taken place in some state and local governments; for example, city managers have discovered that helping their cities to develop economically and socially is more important to their own career success than is concentration upon the effective management of traditional municipal functions.

This appreciation of the role of the civil servant in influencing, formulating, and interpreting policy led a number of schools to initiate course work in some of the major areas of public policy, or to arrange for public administration students to study these subjects in departments of economics, political science and sociology. Thus public administration professors of today teach their students that the government executive has a positive role in the formulation of policy, and, at least at the local levels of government, in community leadership, as well. Appreciation of this evolution has led to a broadening of the curricula in the most innovative schools to emphasize the interrelationships between administration and substantive policy, especially in some of the expanding fields of public service such as urban planning and management, natural resources conservation and management, and economic and social development in the United States and overseas.

Accompanying this concern with policy has been the increase in curricular attention to the problems of complex organization and of human behavior in administrative and organizational settings. The application of systems theory and the use of quantitative methods in decision-making have also become significant features of the educational programs of a number of schools. Much of the stimulus for public administration's interest in these subjects has come from the research in military and in business organizations during and after World War II.

The curricula of U. S. schools have also been enriched through the overseas experiences of faculty members and their contact with the foreign students who flocked to the United States after World War II. These contacts with other cultures brought to the schools of public administration an appreciation of the differences among governmental work situations, and among peoples and societies. Public administration's involvement with the behaviorists was extended; it became concerned with the cultural anthropologists and with the ecologists as well. Lessons learned in cross-cultural operations in a foreign setting brought new insight into the relationships between government and disadvantaged groups on the domestic scene. These new elements have been included in public administration curricula, sometimes initially beginning as special courses, and then as enriching and deepening additions to regular courses and seminars.

The Growth of Interest in World Affairs Aspects of Professional Education

The international aspects of public administration received little attention in U. S. educational institutions prior to World War II. Before that period, the teaching of public administration in U. S. schools was largely confined to the concepts and practices of the U. S. governmental system. Comparative Government was studied in a number of departments of political science but the framework was descriptive, institutional and static. Concern with the dynamics of governmental administration in other nations was largely limited to the personal interest of a few faculty members in the organization and functioning of government in Western European countries.

The relationships in which the United States became involved during the war period required much greater knowledge about the structure and methods of operation of allied, enemy, and neutral governments than had previously concerned U. S. public officials. The relatively few Americans who had had some experience with European public administration were mobilized to train civil affairs officers and civilian administrators and to advise on methods of implementing programs of intergovernmental collaboration. The knowledge of the even smaller number who had had experience with governmental methods in the Far East, or in other exotic areas within the war's ambit, was also pressed into service. Special wartime training programs were established in several universities to prepare U. S. personnel to deal with the administration of liberated or occupied territories.

The initiation of U. S. economic and military aid in the postwar era further expanded the demand for individuals who could deal effectively with the intimate relationships with foreign governmental authorities involved in the administration of large-scale assistance programs and in assisting foreign officials to improve the organization and operation of their countries' public services. As distinguished from the high-level negotiatory and the reportorial roles of traditional diplomatic service, these new activities involved Americans in detailed collaborative work with national planning agencies, with technical ministries, and with provincial and local officials.

Exposure to these new environments and relationships itself provided U. S. aid administrators, and the research-minded public administration scholars who temporarily joined the foreign assistance programs, with opportunities to study the characteristics of administrative systems of foreign countries. Other U. S. faculty members went abroad to teach and do research in public administration at foreign institutions under the Fulbright and similar cultural exchange programs. At a later stage in the development of U. S. economic aid, institutional contracts under which American universities provided technical assistance to foreign governments and educational institutions substantially enlarged the contacts of schools of public administration with governmental structures and methods of administration overseas.

Foreign public administrators and university teachers concerned with education for public service came to the United States schools in substantial numbers for observational visits or to participate in short-term institutes. The development of the postwar system of international organizations also brought

U. S. public administrators and scholars into contact with a variety of governmental systems. Professional organizations, such as the American Society for Public Administration, the Society for International Development and the International Institute of Administrative Sciences (especially its Working Group of Schools and Institutes of Public Administration) encouraged the schools to interest themselves in the world affairs aspects of public administration. All these factors—coupled with the general expansion of the international interests of U. S. scholarship in almost every field—have stimulated the development of a new international dimension in professional education for public administration.

Within the profession, the growing academic interest in the comparative and international side of public administration has been stimulated by the vigorous activities of the Comparative Administration Group (CAG), part of the American Society for Public Administration. This group has advanced active scholarly and practical interest in the international and comparative aspects of administration. For three summers it has brought together faculty members of schools of public administration in seminars which have produced numerous papers containing new insights into selected aspects of the field. In April 1966 it conducted a highly successful conference focusing on development administration and related topics. Its work is already having an impact on curriculum, research, and training programs at a number of institutions. The work of another group, the Committee on Comparative Politics of the Social Science Research Council, has also made significant contributions to knowledge in fields important to public administration. These efforts, both of recent origin, provide an excellent scholarly background for expanded efforts and interest by those concerned with professional schools and programs.

Present Extent of International Involvement

There are great differences in the nature of the international interests and activities of various types of public administration schools. But almost all of them have been affected by the expansion of governmental and private relationships with public administration systems of other nations, and by the growth of personal contacts between U. S. practitioners, teachers and researchers, and their foreign colleagues.

At one end of the spectrum, the limited number of schools or programs which specialize in the preparation of practitioners for local government and in part-time courses for persons already employed in domestic public services appear to have introduced relatively little international content into their programs. Even in these institutions, however, there appears to be growing interest in such subjects as the worldwide problems of urbanism and metropolitan development and their possible implications for Americans concerned with analogous questions in the United States.

At the other end of the range are the schools, such as Harvard and Princeton, in which public administration—in the traditional sense of the study of governmental operations—appears subordinated to the study of public policy. Possibly because international problems have become, within very recent years, such a pervasive concern of U. S. public policy, and possibly because schools of this type tend to have a heavy interdisciplinary emphasis, this group appears to be very broadly concerned with world affairs studies and research. Schools which specialize in international affairs, such as the Fletcher School of Law and Diplomacy at Tufts and the School of Advanced International Studies at Johns Hopkins, also fall into this general category.

In the middle is a third group of schools which offers broad generic public administration preparation for practitioners and train researchers and teachers in this field. While these schools are concerned with public policy, their primary emphasis is upon the operational aspects of policy formulation and program execution. They are increasingly interested in teaching and research in development administration and are also devoting attention to the organization and administration of national and multilateral machinery for the conduct of international relations. Schools of this type tend to be more heavily involved in overseas institutional projects than are those in the other two groups. They also accept the bulk of the foreign students in public administration and provide short-term training for foreign officials. Pittsburgh, Southern California and Syracuse are examples of this type of institution.

World Affairs Content of Curricula

The opportunities for instructors and research-minded scholars to become familiar with many countries and international organizations have brought a new fund of international knowledge to American schools. Descriptive, analytical, and comparative studies have appeared in increasing volume in professional journals; these have been followed by case histories, monographs and books. This body of teaching materials has enabled the schools to introduce the study of the administrative systems of other countries into courses and curricula previously limited to U. S.—or, at best, to American and Western European—content. The result has been a widespread increase in the international content of public administration programs.

The appearance of large numbers of foreign students, foreign scholars, and visiting foreign officials on the campuses of U. S. schools further stimulated the introduction of international materials into the public administration curricula. Many instructors soon recognized that courses which dealt only with U. S. or Western European public administration were of limited value to students who came from quite different cultures. This further stimulated the development of teaching materials designed both to acquaint U. S. students with the realities of public administration in other societies and to aid foreign students in understanding the application of professional concepts to the situations in their own countries.

Substantial contributions to the development of the international curricula and teaching materials of schools of public administration have come from other professions and academic disciplines. The formulation of national and regional development plans has required new types of collaboration between the economic, social, and other planners and the public administrators who must implement the programs and projects contemplated in these plans. Agricultural extension, rural public health, and rural education have provided experience and new concepts about the organization and operation of rural development programs. Political science, economics, sociology, cultural anthropology, and social psychology have thrown light on many aspects of public administration in both our own society and in other nations.

Two methods have been used to introduce international content into public administration curricula. Some schools have emphasized the inclusion of comparative and cross-cultural teaching in basic courses. World affairs elements have been introduced both into generic courses dealing with broad administrative concepts and public policy issues, and into more specialized functional courses in such fields as personnel administration, financial administration and administrative analysis. Cases and problems illustrating administrative methods and administrative behavior in foreign environments are used to introduce students to other systems. Attention is also devoted to the ecology of public administration and to the implications of societal modernization upon the character of governmental services. Southern California has been especially noteworthy in this regard, but a number of other schools are also placing special emphasis upon this type of teaching.

The principal advantage of this plan is that it provides the general run of students with at least an initial exposure to the international aspects of his profession and acquaints him with the existence of both similarities and differences in professional values, concepts and methods as between his own culture and foreign ones. It suffers from the disadvantage of requiring that instructors in a variety of different subjects also have experience and competence in dealing with the international aspects of their specializations. Moreover, appropriate comparative and cross-cultural teaching materials are still limited.

An alternative arrangement is that of establishing distinctive international courses, such as "Comparative Administration" in which the instructor covers the international aspects of a wide range of public administration subjects. A broad spectrum of schools offer courses of this character; the list includes Alabama, American University, George Washington, Minnesota, Kansas, New York University and the University of California at Los Angeles. This type of curriculum requires fewer instructors with substantial international experience, but it demands that they cover exceedingly wide ranges of subject matter, with the consequent dangers of superficial treatment of some aspects. Moreover, this approach usually means that only a limited part of the student body is introduced to the international aspects of its profession.

Operational Relevance of International Curricula

Since they seek to prepare the great preponderance of their students as practitioners, most schools of public administration emphasize the application of public administration principles in problem-solving contexts, rather than as abstract doctrines. The schools generally have placed similar stress upon the operational implications of the international aspects of their curricula. This has been reflected in some of the new courses developed in certain institutions.

The schools which accentuate public policy appear to rely heavily upon courses in such disciplinary subjects as international relations, international economics and history, and upon area study programs, as a method of introducing international content into their curricula. These courses add valuable knowledge to the student's background but they usually lack the operational relevance which characterizes education for public administration.

An operational linkage has been supplied through the courses which several schools have developed in the administration of international activities. Thus Syracuse and Pittsburgh underline the relationship between policy and administration in courses dealing with the processes of formulating foreign policy and with the organization and administration of U. S. overseas operations. The operational problems of regional integration, such as those involved in Europe and in Latin America, are also studied in some schools of public administration. Many schools, including Maryland, New York University, Utah, George Washington, the University of California at Los Angeles, and Ohio State, provide opportunities for study of the programs, organization and administration of international agencies.

The study of development administration is a relatively recent innovation, and only a limited number of schools—principally Michigan, Indiana, Pittsburgh, Southern California and Syracuse—offer course work in this field. Development administration focuses upon the problems of government organization and administration in countries which are seeking to accelerate their economic growth and upon the methods of bringing about the administrative improvements required for the operation of development programs. The planning and execution of development involves the fostering of societal changes, the massive mobilization of resources and their allocation to a wide range of development projects and activities, and the coordination of public and private effort. The scope of this subject matter is substantially broader than traditional public administration; courses in development administration usually are taught as part of a more comprehensive program in economic and social development of low-income countries.

Courses in cross-cultural operations are another recent development designed for students with special interest in the international aspects of their profession. Drawing upon a number of disciplines, especially cultural anthropology, and transactional and social psychology, these courses are being used to help equip students to deal with the operational aspects of programs involving the interaction of individuals of differing cultural backgrounds. Southern California has been introducing content of this character into some of its courses in development administration, and Michigan State has been including a strong behavioral element in its special training programs for foreign officials. Pittsburgh, in addition to offering regular cross-cultural operations courses, has also been experimenting with the adaptation of sensitivity-training techniques in short-term programs designed to aid mature participants (and their wives) to develop insight into the interpersonal and intergroup relationships which occur in cross-cultural transactions. American University also offers work in this field.

The Need for Curricular Research

The rapid growth of interest in the world affairs aspects of public administration and the urgency of training students for international work has required much of the teaching in this field to be developed out of empirical experience rather than through the scientific accumulation of knowledge. Systematic, comprehensive exploration of administrative concepts, processes and behavior in other countries, especially as they relate to problems of political, economic and social development, is a high priority for schools of public administration. Broadening and improving of teaching, as well as more effective performance in institutional activities overseas, is heavily dependent upon greatly increased attention to research in depth to enlarge the understanding of the administrative systems of other countries produced by the pioneer studies. Three broad types of research activities seem worthy of special attention.

First, many more descriptive and analytical case studies of administrative institutions and processes in the developing areas should be added to the literature. Increasingly, these should be truly comparative in approach and related to theories of administrative behavior, organization and even whole systems.

A second research activity should be the stimulation of research on administration by teachers and scholars of other countries. Much more research related to bureaucracies, organizations, and operations in foreign countries is needed and much more could be done by indigenous scholars than is now the case. Professional schools in this country should encourage foreign scholars and assist in the development of new research institutes abroad. The contributions of U. S. scholars which presently predominate in this field should eventually represent only a small part of the total expansion of knowledge in public administration.

A third activity might well be intensified attention to research on administrative change and development. Analyses of the functioning of bureaucracies in various settings; analytical and comparative studies of institution-building as a strategy or as a process; studies of various aspects of the administration of development-oriented programs; analyses of cross-cultural and international assistance efforts in various fields—these and many other research tasks should be approached in the immediate future.

It would be unwise to urge limits or sharply to define research priorities at this stage of our knowledge. Too much is still to be done. There is, as yet, no general theory to guide the educational effort. What is needed now is a major expansion of research, with the resulting accumulation of new knowledge of many diverse areas and on a wide range of subjects important to public administration.

Some Special Aspects of World Affairs Involvement

The Impact of Foreign Students and Officials

The most recent published figures for foreign students in the United States[7] indicate that, in the academic year 1965-66, out of a total of almost 83,000 foreign students, only 473 were in the field of public administration. This is a lower proportion than in any of the other major professional fields, although it is only slightly less than for law. In contrast, there were over 18,000 foreign engineering students, almost 8,000 in business administration, more than 4,000 educators, and about an equal number in the medical sciences.

All of the larger schools of public administration had foreign students enrolled in 1965-66. Non-Americans made up over 30 percent of the student body at Harvard and at Pittsburgh. Cornell, Michigan, Missouri, and New York University each reported that foreign students represented from 10 to 20 percent of their enrollment.

U. S. schools of public administration are apparently becoming somewhat more selective about the foreign students they admit. The novelty of the exotic seems to have worn off and most schools have recognized that accepting an inadequately prepared applicant merely because he is a foreigner may not only create problems for the institution, but often may also result in personal tragedy for the student. However, both the Agency for International Development and the United Nations still sometimes urge schools to accept students sponsored by their field missions who are substantially below the academic or linguistic standards required for successful academic performance.

The foreign students in U. S. schools of public administration fall into three major groups. The first consists of undergraduates or graduate students who have not had previous work experience. Some of these students have come to the United States directly from secondary schools or undergraduate colleges in their own countries. Their career plans often are vague and sometimes quite unrealistic. While many of them are able to maintain a satisfactory standard of academic performance, the majority have some difficulty in keeping up with the required level of work. In part, this reflects language handicaps which often are a major trouble even among students from countries in which English is the normal language of instruction. Some of the problems are attributable to the students' unfamiliarity, not only with the U. S. governmental system, but also with public administration in their own countries. Few of them have had the basic social science courses which provide much of the foundation for U. S. professional education.

Most of these foreign students are able to earn the degree for which they have enrolled, but in some instances the degree appears to have been granted almost on compassionate grounds, when an American student with a comparable level of performance would be failed. Generally, the schools seem to be reaching the conclusion that a foreign student who has not had work experience in the governmental system of his own country is not likely to secure benefits from a public administration program in a U. S. school commensurate with the real costs of providing this instruction.

A second, and larger, group of foreign students are those who come to U. S. institutions after they have completed their undergraduate work in their own countries or elsewhere and, in addition, have had several years of experience in their own governmental services. Students in this class are usually somewhat older than the first group; normally they are on educational leave from middle management posts in their national administration. Most of them look forward to their U. S. experience as preparation for further progress on the ladder of advancement. They have professional and personal roots in their own societies. Students in this category ordinarily are better prepared and more strongly motivated for professional study than their less-experienced compatriots.

While they suffer from the same inadequacies in English and in the social sciences and lack of familiarity with U. S. government and U. S. pedagogical methods as the younger group, they normally have greater capacity for relating public administration theory and practice to their own experience. Their knowledge of the administrative systems of their own governments helps them to participate in seminars and discussion groups and thus enables them to make positive contributions to the comparison of different systems. In many cases these foreign students have a more sophisticated understanding of the political institutions and other institutions of their countries than some American students possess about those of the United States. These more mature foreign students generally secure greater benefits from their work in U. S. schools than do the inexperienced group.

The third category of foreign students are those who are seeking higher degrees from U. S. institutions, either at the master's or the doctoral level, to enable them to teach public administration in their own countries. This is a relatively small group; members tend to cluster in the U. S. schools which have long-term relationships with overseas universities, schools and institutes. Many of them lack the extensive preparation in the social sciences which U. S. schools customarily expect of most of their own aspirants for faculty posts, and relatively few have had practitioner experience in their own countries. These deficiencies often make the task of equipping them for teaching assignments in their home institutions an exceedingly difficult one. Nevertheless, because of its multiplier potential, the education of these future faculty members usually represents one of the most effective contributions a school in the United States can make.

Foreign students add an international flavor to a school and bring some U. S. students into contact with individuals of another culture for the first time, but their presence does not of itself necessarily increase the international content of the school's program. There are indications that the enrollment of foreign students has not affected the curricula or teaching methods of a number of schools; in several institutions with substantial numbers of such students the course work continues to center almost exclusively upon U. S. concepts and practices. In some schools of this character there seems to be little evidence of special assistance to help foreign students relate American doctrines and techniques to the quite different backgrounds of their own countries.

Other schools make intensive efforts to provide foreign students with a meaningful educational experience and also to obtain for their American students the benefits of cross-cultural exposure. These schools include teaching materials about different systems of public administration in their curricula and relate these systems on a comparative basis to the political, economic, social, and cultural backgrounds of the countries concerned. Some of them make special efforts through academic counseling to assist foreigners to comprehend the history and ecology of U. S. public administration and the problems of adapting and introducing new concepts and technologies into systems that are resistant to change. Several schools place stress upon small seminars as a major method of instruction, emphasizing that this technique facilitates the participation of foreign students (as well as their American fellows) in class discussion. These schools also employ working parties made up of both foreign and U. S. students as "syndicates" for the study of specific problems or cases as a method of bringing the two groups into a common experience.

A number of U. S. schools of public administration require their graduate students to complete a period of work experience under an internship in a public agency, either as an alternative or in addition to a master's thesis. The placement of the foreign student in such an internship often presents a special problem, especially if he has language difficulties and lacks familiarity with U. S. methods of work and with the mores of U. S. administration. Participation of the school's own faculty in the supervision of the foreign student's work usually results in a more successful internship experience than is the case when the supervision is left to a busy public official who, despite his goodwill and personal interest, may have neither the time nor the capacity for the requisite counseling and interpretation. Internship placements with international agencies, whose staffs are multinational and whose administrative methods are somewhat eclectic, often also are quite successful. Unfortunately, they are difficult for most schools to arrange.

As a result of their experience in providing orientation concerning U. S. public administration to foreign visitors brought to the United States for brief observation tours under governmental technical assistance or cultural relations programs, several schools have developed special institutes or other short-term training programs for foreign officials on specific aspects of administrative doctrine and practice. In some ways these are an international extension of the in-service training and executive development activities which several schools have long provided for public officials from their own localities.

While these short-term training activities undoubtedly are of value to foreign officials who cannot be away from their posts long enough to undertake regular course work, their educational impact necessarily is limited. This is particularly the case where the training period extends only over a few weeks and the visiting group consists of individuals of different nationalities and different levels of experience. The most effective short-term programs appear to be those which focus on limited, specific aspects of administration reasonably related to the present or potential job responsibilities of the foreign participants. The brief duration requires that instructors in such programs have an especially good understanding of the environment and the administrative system from which their students come. Michigan State, Southern California, Syracuse and Pittsburgh have been especially innovative in developing programs of this character.

Almost all schools report that their foreign students and officials are afforded opportunities to observe American home and community life. The extent and nature of planned activities in this field varies greatly and there are indications that foreign students in large urban centers may have more limited activity of this nature than those in smaller cities. Much of the exposure of these students to community and family life in the United States appears to take place in relatively prosperous middle-class environment. Few foreign students are provided with firsthand contact with the circumstances, problems and attitudes of low-income groups in our society.

Overseas Experience for U. S. Students

Academic programs in comparative administration, administration of economic development, international administration, cross-cultural operations, and other elements of training for the international aspects of public administration—even when they include close collaboration with foreign students and distinguished foreign scholars—still represent a limited type of preparation for dealing with the problems encountered by practitioners. For the student who has decided to specialize in the international aspects of the profession, work experience in an overseas setting can add a realistic appreciation of the differences between domestic and international activities and provide him with opportunities for testing out some of the concepts and hypotheses he has been considering in his scholastic work.

The type of overseas internship assignments which can furnish experience of this nature unfortunately are expensive. However, nongovernmental foundations have provided funds to support several programs under which a small number of U. S. public administration students or recent graduates are placed in overseas work in foreign governments, in international agencies, or in offices of U. S. government agencies abroad. The selection of these interns, their placement, and their supervision place heavy loads upon the schools involved, but the experience of these programs has been highly successful.

Another type of overseas assignment has been developed by some schools which are engaged in assistance to foreign educational institutions; the AID or foundation contracts under which these activities are financed usually permit the employment of U. S. graduate assistants for service at the overseas school. Customarily, these assistants aid U. S. faculty members in research projects. These arrangements may be less productive of practitioner skills for dealing in a foreign environment than are work assignments in an operating agency overseas. They can, however, provide students with valuable experience and permit some development of their personal potential for overseas and cross-cultural service.

Many U. S. schools have admitted returning Peace Corps Volunteers for graduate study in public administration, in some cases with fellowships through the Ford Foundation-financed program for Peace Corps veterans. The overseas experience of these students has preceded their professional education and the tasks which most of them undertook in Peace Corps service usually involved somewhat less complex administrative situations than are desirable in an internship program. These students, nevertheless, usually are able to apply their foreign experience meaningfully in their academic work. After completion of their studies, a number of them have returned to public administration activities overseas in AID missions, in international agencies or in other organizations.

Overseas Institutional Activities

An important area of institutional overseas involvement of U. S. schools of public administration is their participation in technical assistance projects financed under the U. S. foreign aid program. As of June 30, 1966, six schools[8] were engaged in contractual arrangements under which they were sending faculty to schools and institutes of public administration in low-income countries. While these U. S. faculty members often teach courses in the foreign institution, their primary responsibility usually is to aid in improving the organization, curriculum, teaching methods and other aspects of the foreign schools' program. These arrangements often also include provisions for faculty members, or prospective faculty members, of the foreign school to come to the U. S. institution for advanced study. In several instances, public administration is only one element in a more comprehensive contract under which an American university provides technical assistance to an overseas one in a number of fields of study. A few contracts of a somewhat similar character have been financed by the Ford Foundation.

Although U. S. schools of public administration have had over a decade of experience with these institutional contracts, opinion is sharply divided among the schools as to whether this type of activity represents a sound educational investment. A smaller number of U. S. schools are involved in these arrangements than was the case a few years ago. Contracts in public administration represented only about 4 percent of the total number, and about 3 percent of the total dollar value, of university technical assistance contracts financed by AID in June 1966. In some instances U. S. institutions have taken the initiative in deciding not to continue a contract after the expiration of an initial three-year period. In other cases, political changes in the overseas country, shifts in the emphasis of the aid program, or unsatisfactory performance either by the U. S. school or by its indigenous counterpart have led to the termination of the contract.

During the first years of the use of the university contract technique, some of the arrangements for work with foreign institutions had not been carefully considered by the governmental authorities involved or by either the foreign or the U. S. school. Objectives, terms, and methods of operation sometimes were extremely vague. More recently the planning, negotiation, and operation of contracts of this type have been improved. There seem to be fewer complaints from U. S. institutions about excessive governmental controls and similar aspects of contractual relationships, although some schools report continuing difficulties.

More fundamental issues involve the question of the value of such contracts to the U. S. school. Some schools maintain that they involve an undue diversion of scarce faculty talent to the detriment of teaching and research on the home campus. There is skepticism about the actual extent of "feedback" from the overseas experience of faculty and its relevancy to the basic educational program of the American institution. Schools generally point to this as one of the major problems of overseas operations. If many of the U. S. faculty members who go abroad are only temporarily members of the U. S. school's permanent staff, and do not return to teach at that institution, the possibilities of using these contracts to increase the international dimensions of the curriculum on the home campus are limited.

Some schools believe that many of the benefits which their institutions might secure from contracts can also be achieved by leaves of absence to individual faculty members to undertake research and teaching assignments overseas. In this connection they point out that government-financed technical assistance relationships are limited to less-developed, low-income countries and that many of the most interesting developments in public administration are in economically more advanced nations.

On the other hand, there is general agreement that these contracts have usually helped to initiate significant improvements in public administration education in the overseas countries, and that this represents an important international service activity for U. S. professional schools. There is also consensus that these overseas assignments have provided valuable opportunities for the development of the international backgrounds of younger faculty of U. S. schools. Much research in comparative administration and much of the increased understanding of the behavioral and ecological aspects of public administration and of the complex nature of cross-cultural operations has come out of the experience of U. S. faculty members under these contracts. The potential faculty members of overseas schools who have studied at U. S. institutions as part of these arrangements have usually enriched the U. S. faculty's international understanding. They also have returned to their own countries with enhanced competence in their professional field, and usually with favorable attitudes toward U. S. concepts of professional education in public administration.

There obviously is validity in both of these viewpoints. U. S. schools which have—or can obtain—financial resources to provide international experience for their faculty and graduate students from sources more flexible than governmental technical assistance contracts are in a different situation from those for which this type of arrangement represents the principal possibility for overseas institutional involvement. For the latter group of schools, the first flush of enthusiasm is over; additional commitments are being examined with more circumspection and more careful attention to the opportunity costs than was the case a few years ago. The development of collaborative arrangements or consortia, under which several schools of public administration collaborate in assisting one or more foreign institutions, is a possible approach to ease the burden which a single school is usually required to carry under the present pattern. Arrangements of this character have already been instituted in connection with a number of university-to-university contracts in other fields.

Several of the most experienced U. S. schools have come to the conclusion that they should concentrate their major international effort of an institutional character upon assistance in the establishment of indigenous public administration schools or institutes overseas which ultimately will be able to train most of the administrators required in a country or a region. They consider that this represents a sounder use of their own resources than is achieved by the admission of large numbers of practitioner-level foreign students on their home campuses. At the same time they recognize that successful performance of an institution-to-institution arrangement requires the U. S. school to make a heavy investment of scarce faculty and administrative talent and this can only be achieved if there is a real commitment, not only by the professional school and its faculty, but also by the university of which it is a part.

A serious limitation upon the ability of schools which wish to aid in the development of overseas institutions is the shortage of faculty members who are competent to do effective work abroad. As is true for U. S. higher education in general, the number of persons who are qualified to teach in public administration programs at the graduate level is far below the demand. The expansion of governmental activities and the differentials between governmental (especially federal) salaries and university renumeration afford severe competition for both present faculty and for individuals who might consider academic careers. Even if schools are able to overcome the problem of training faculty for their basic domestic programs, they must still face the additional difficulty of preparing faculty for overseas service. This may require a liberal leave policy to enable younger instructors to undertake temporary governmental employment abroad; to engage in internationally related research, or to participate in cultural exchange programs. Eventually, this type of preparation and experience may become a norm for all public administration faculty; but for the immediate future, schools must appreciate the costs involved in equipping themselves to undertake institutional projects of this character.

Most of the overseas research on international aspects of public administration involves individual faculty, rather than institutional activity. However, institutional technical assistance contracts are making it possible for faculty members of these schools to devote part of their time overseas to research work and to secure the services of graduate assistants to help in research projects. Some research work of this character, such as that of the Inter-University Research Program in Institution Building (whose member institutions are the University of Pittsburgh, Indiana University, Michigan State University and Syracuse University), is also being financed by AID research contracts with U. S. schools. The grants which the Ford Foundation has made to augment the international dimensions of a number of U. S. universities are also providing support for some faculty research on international aspects of public administration.

Strategies for Introducing a World Affairs Emphasis

The introduction of world affairs content into the program of a school of public administration usually represents an institutional decision to emphasize the international element, rather than to expand in some other aspect of the field. Even if additional resources are available to finance the faculty and other costs involved in the new international interest, some part of the school's existing activity inevitably will receive less attention. Acceptance of the new emphasis requires the development of a conscious strategy to overcome the inertia, and possibly the resistance, which such an innovation often encounters.

The environment of the school, and of its parent university, is a key determinant of such a strategy. The administrators and faculty members who desire to bring about such a change must take into account the generally accepted concept of their school's purpose and its philosophy of public administration. They must consider the extent to which faculty interest is widespread, deep and genuine. They must estimate how much support, how much indifference, and how much opposition, the introduction of this new aspect will encounter in other parts of the university and among trustees.

The process and mechanism by which goals and strategies are formulated will differ from school to school. In most institutions a faculty committee or seminar would be the primary mechanism to examine such matters as the current level of faculty and student interest, the existing courses and other activities relevant to the development of the school's international dimension, the goals which might be established and the ways in which a world affairs emphasis might be initiated. This group may also serve as a channel for securing the support of faculty members from other parts of the university who may be interested in expanding the international concerns of the institution.

At an early stage in its planning the school should come to at least a tentative conclusion concerning the level of international involvement it considers desirable and feasible in the near future. Given the pluralistic nature of professional education in public administration, a wide range of differing degrees of world affairs interest and of subject-matter emphasis is inevitable.

Within this broad spectrum, there appear to be two basic types of situations. In one group are those schools which presently have little or no international involvement but which have decided that at least a minimum acquaintanceship with the world affairs aspects of the profession is required for the preparation of a competent practitioner. At the other end of the range are the schools which already have embodied significant international elements in their programs and have decided to equip some of their students as practitioners, teachers, or researchers who specialize in internationally related work.

The first level would seem to be within the capabilities of any school which offers a graduate professional degree in public administration. The second requires a heavy investment of scarce resources and may be feasible only for a small number of institutions which are able to provide the specialized faculty and the other facilities and services involved in an international program of some depth.

Recommendations

This study has indicated need for more and better international content in the preparation of public administrators for service at home and abroad. It has also noted the interest of students, faculty, and administrators in accelerating progress in this direction, and the successful experimentation and achievements of several of the most innovative institutions. Against this background, and recognizing the pluralism and the differences among public administration programs, the Task Force considers that, as a minimum, all schools should provide their students with understanding of those world affairs elements that are basic to the concept of professional education in the last third of the twentieth century. Beyond these, it suggests a range of additional activities appropriate for those schools which decide to include in their programs a specialization in the international aspects of public administration.

1. At a minimal level, all schools must face the problem of how to equip their graduates, not only with capability for practice of the profession but also with a breadth of understanding of the society in which they will carry on this practice. In today's interdependent world, this means that individuals entering the profession of public administration must be acquainted with:

—the impact of world affairs, of the developments and trends in other lands, and of this nation's relations with other countries upon the society and the economy in which we live;
—the effect of differing cultures, differing philosophies, and differing physical environments upon the theory and the practice of public administration.

2. These minimal objectives require the progressive deepening and enriching of the present public administration curricula. The needed changes are not revolutionary, but they involve significant widening of horizons. The additional emphasis should focus upon comparing and contrasting values, institutions, and the operations of public agencies in this country and in other lands, and in international organizations, so as to provide the student with a fuller appreciation of the theory and practice in the disciplines and subject matter areas encompassed in the study of public administration. Students should also be encouraged to develop and maintain proficiency in one or more of the major foreign languages. The incorporation of such international materials in course offerings can aid the student to understand the ecological factors which have influenced administrative organization and practices in all countries.

3. *To enable its faculty to provide this enriched curriculum, the school must encourage its faculty members to locate opportunities through which they may study and obtain broadened experience in the practice of their specialized skills overseas.* These opportunities may be found in foreign research and travel grants available through government or the foundations. This type of wider experience may also be obtained through the participation of faculty members in projects involving the development of professional schools overseas, under the auspices of their own university or of another institution. Special efforts will be required to identify opportunities through which junior faculty members may achieve an understanding of the international aspects of their specializations. The foreign language competence of faculty should be strengthened.

The expansion of the number of faculty members with deepened appreciation of the practice of their professions in other cultures must be accompanied by the establishment or extension of techniques by which their interest and their new understanding may be communicated to other members of the faculty of the school. Schools should also encourage the ordered and persistent exchange of ideas among faculty with foreign experience in several disciplines so as to illuminate the effects of the cultural setting and the differing institutional and physical environments on the theory and practice of the profession.

4. *As an additional method of enriching its program, at even the minimal level, each school of public administration should also bring to its classrooms:*

—*visiting foreign scholars and practitioners already in the United States;*
—*such foreign nationals as it can accommodate in its student body.*

The association of foreign scholars, practitioners, and students with the Americans who are preparing for the profession can constitute a meaningful element in developing the broadened view that is the hallmark of the professional man.

5. Above this minimum of international content there are increasing levels of world affairs involvement. Only a very few U. S. schools are now significantly committed to—and capable of—the preparation of students for internationally related public service in the federal government, in multilateral agencies, and in other organizations associated with the world affairs aspects of public administration. More well-trained men and women are required for

these functions and more well-equipped schools are needed to prepare them.

The urgent need is for the development of at least eight or ten carefully chosen U. S. schools of public administration with substantial competence in international educational, research and service activities. The schools which decide to make the world affairs aspects of public administration a major component of their programs have a more complex task than those which undertake only to enrich their curricula as a means of broadening the international understanding of their student bodies. They will need to add substantial depth and specialization in their course work. This will require a large, diversified and widely experienced faculty, development of new teaching materials, comprehensive library and language facilities, and programs of overseas research and relationships with foreign educational institutions.

6. *The key task of this group of U. S. schools is the preparation of practitioners for internationally focused operational work and of teachers and researchers both for U. S. institutions and for public administration schools and training programs in foreign countries.* While there is general recognition of the need for substantial increases in the supply of such personnel, there has been almost no long-range planning which would indicate the specific skills which are likely to be in greatest demand or the regions of the world for which language and other specialized training may be required. This is a task which should be undertaken cooperatively by the federal government, representatives of the professional schools, and foundations interested in this field.

7. *Upon the basis of this type of analysis and planning and of proposals submitted by the schools which already have demonstrated competence in internationally related work and are willing to commit themselves to further major efforts, the federal government—presumably through the new Center for Educational Cooperation—should, over a period of time, select a limited number of institutions for major encouragement and aid.* Each of these schools might specialize, either in a principal aspect of world affairs activity or in a geographic region. To fulfill their responsibilities for providing the numbers and types of qualified individuals, the selected schools should:

   a. augment and intensify their course work in such areas as comparative administration, administration of international programs, development administration and cross-cultural operations, and in the international aspects of other supporting professions and disciplines. In some instances, this will involve the addition of new subjects to the school's curriculum; in others it will require a new international emphasis in the teaching of present subjects; in still others it will necessitate the establishment or strengthening of joint programs between the school of public administration and other professional schools and disciplinary departments;

b. institute an organized program for facilitating the contribution of the school's faculty to the development of urgently needed conceptual frameworks, comparative research, case studies, and other teaching material concerning the international aspects of the profession. This would include grants-in-aid to U. S. and visiting foreign faculty and liberal institutional policies concerning sabbaticals for research and writing purposes;

c. expand library facilities to provide comprehensive coverage of world affairs matters of professional concern and maximize collaboration with other libraries in the same or related fields. In subject areas of special interest to the school, efforts should be made to develop the library's character as a depository;

d. enter into institutional relationships with one or several parallel schools in foreign countries, under which a reciprocal exchange of faculty members is maintained, collaborative research and institutional development activities undertaken, and opportunities provided for exchange of students, especially those engaged in postgraduate study. These relationships usually are most productive if they are part of a comprehensive university-to-university arrangement. Some of these arrangements, especially with institutions in economically advanced countries, may be partly financed upon an exchange basis, but additional funds will usually be required for travel and other costs. AID-financed contracts with institutions in developing countries lack some of the desirable flexibility but they can serve as a valuable resource for providing both faculty and graduate students cross-cultural experience overseas, and as a source of home campus "feedback" to enrich curricula;

e. bring foreign professors and scholars to the school to give courses, special seminars, and school-wide lectures in their fields of professional competence and to participate in the development of curricula and teaching materials. Schools might also seek the participation of younger foreign scholars in research projects, especially those involving collaboration with their own younger faculty members or graduate students;

f. establish, either on an elective or a required basis, overseas internships enabling students to observe and—if possible—to participate in the professional work of foreign governments or international organizations. The overseas internship program of the Maxwell School at Syracuse (at the master's level) is an illustration of this type of activity. The experience in the field of business administration of the Association Internationale des Etudiants en Sciences Economiques et Commerciales (AIESEC) in arranging for the exchange of summer work opportunities overseas also suggests a possible technique which might be applied in public administration;

g. assist governmental agencies to fulfill their responsibilities for the continuing education of their own personnel. In-service training of experienced U. S. and foreign professional personnel, both in regular degree programs and in special short-term institutes, enables a school to contribute to the competence of individuals who are already engaged in professional practice. These practitioners often bring the values and problems of their current experiences to the campus and serve as a source of stimulation to faculty and other students.

8. *Substantial resources will be required to meet the costs of the general enrichment of the curricula of all schools and for the new or expanded programs and facilities of the limited number of schools which will develop special international capabilities.* The requirements will differ from institution to institution, but in general they will include the costs of faculty expansion and development; of fellowships, especially for U. S. students; of research projects, especially those involving the development of teaching materials; and, in many instances, of additional library and classroom facilities.

a. At least part of the costs of producing graduates who are well qualified in the international aspects of public administration should be met by the governmental authorities whose demands for these skills far exceed the present capacity of the schools to fulfill them. Existing federal government programs, such as AID, those in educational and cultural exchange, and National Defense Education Act Fellowships, may supply a limited part of the requisite financing. The grants to universities for international centers specified in the International Education Act of 1966 may also assist.

b. Producing an adequate number of public administration graduates with special preparation for internationally related work is part of the more general problem of augmenting the supply of professionally trained public administrators. A general program of federal fellowships in public administration, with supplements to the institution to help meet the difference between tuition charges and actual educational costs (comparable to the fellowships which are already provided in other professional fields where personnel shortages are a matter of national concern) is essential to enable the schools to provide the numbers of well-equipped public administrators required for increasingly complex governmental functions, at home and overseas.

c. Major philanthropic institutions should continue, as in the past, to aid professional schools—and their respective parent universities—to develop their international programs and activities. Some of the smaller local civic, service or nationality-oriented foundations have financed specific projects, such as fellowships for foreign students, travel grants for U. S. faculty and students, visits by distinguished lecturers, and library expansion. The interest of these and other community sources of assistance should continue to be elicited.

Notes

[1] This "jointness" has been extended further at at least one institution. The Irvine campus of the University of California is experimenting with a School of Administration, generically considered, covering educational as well as public and business administration.

[2] Ward Stewart, *Graduate Study in Public Administration*, Washington, D.C.: Government Printing Office, 1961.
Other studies in education for public administration worth noting here include: International Institute of Administrative Sciences, *Education for Development Administration*, 1967; Ward Stewart and John C. Honey, *University-Sponsored Executive Development Programs in the Public Service*, 1966; Stephen B. Sweeney (ed.), *Education for Administrative Careers in Government Service*, 1958; Dwight Waldo, *The Study of Public Administration*, 1955; Edward W. Weidner, *Technical Assistance in Public Administration Overseas: The Case for Development Administration*, 1964.

[3] These were: American University, Harvard, New York University, Pittsburgh, Princeton, Puerto Rico, Southern California, State University of New York, Syracuse, and the University of Washington as schools of public administration or public affairs; and Arizona, City College of New York, Cornell, Missouri, and Pennsylvania as schools which included both business administration and public administration.

[4] See Department of Health, Education, and Welfare, U. S. Office of Education, *Earned Degrees Conferred 1963-64: Bachelor's and Higher Degrees*, Washington, D.C.: Government Printing Office, 1966 and previous years.

[5] The figures collected by the Council on Graduate Education in Public Administration for the years 1964-65 and 1965-66 show an increase of about 20 percent in the number of Master's degrees earned, as compared with the Office of Education report for 1963-64. They also indicate a total of 635 students enrolled in doctoral-level programs in public administration, an increase of approximately 30 percent over the Office of Education's figures for 1963-64.

[6] Ward Stewart, *op cit.*, p. 21.

[7] *Open Doors, 1966*, New York: Institute of International Education.

[8] These were: Southern California (in Pakistan); Michigan (in India); Syracuse (in Kenya); Pittsburgh (in Nigeria and Ecuador); Cornell (in Turkey); and Harvard (in Chile). An interesting contract for assistance to the National Institute of Development Administration in Thailand, combining public administration with economics and several other fields has recently been undertaken by the Midwest Universities Consortium for International Activities (Illinois, Michigan State, Indiana and Wisconsin).

Selected Bibliography

(Compiled by Alice Tetelman, Research Assistant)

Comparative Administration Group. American Society for Public Administration. *Development Administration.* Report by a Special Committee. Bloomington, Indiana: Comparative Administration Group, in care of International Development Research Center, Indiana University, 1964. (CAG Occasional Papers).

International Institute of Administrative Sciences. *Education for Development Administration.* Brussels: The Institute, 1967.

Molitor, Andre. *Public Administration.* Paris: Unesco, The University Teaching of Social Sciences Series, 1959.

Robinson, Mary E. *Education for Social Change: Establishing Institutes of Public and Business Administration Abroad.* Washington, D.C.: The Brookings Institution, 1961.

Stewart, Ward. *Graduate Study in Public Administration.* Washington, D.C.: Government Printing Office, 1961.

———— and John C. Honey. *University-Sponsored Executive Development Programs in the Public Service.* Washington, D.C.: Government Printing Office, 1966.

Stone, Donald C. *Education in Public Administration.* Brussels: International Institute of Administrative Sciences, 1963. .

Symposium on Research Needs Regarding the Development of Administrative Capabilities in Emerging Countries. *Prepared Papers and Report on Proceedings.* Conducted for the Agency for International Development by The Brookings Institution, November 14-17, 1965. Washington, D.C.: The Institution, n.d.

Weidner, Edward W. *Technical Assistance in Public Administration Overseas: The Case for Development Administration.* Chicago: Public Administration Service, 1964.

THE U. S. PROFESSIONAL SCHOOL
CONFRONTS THE WORLD*

THE UNIQUENESS OF THE U. S. PROFESSIONAL SCHOOL

The professional school, as found on the U. S. university campus, is unique. No other country combines preparation for careers in agriculture, business administration, aeronautical engineering, social work, and medical technology under the same university umbrella which also shelters the traditional learned professions of law, medicine, and theology, as well as the humanities and sciences. The preparation of all practitioners for all the clearly recognized professions is a university responsibility only in the United States. Even here, this is a recent twentieth-century development which deviates from the earlier European models.

Professional curricula in the United States reflect their university home base in that they characteristically include a variety of liberalizing, nonprofessional courses, often taught by the faculty in the college of liberal arts. This is particularly the situation where the professional training is at the undergraduate level, but also holds true at the graduate level where the behavioral and social sciences are increasingly being introduced to provide insight into problems of professional practice in the community.

The professional schools also manifest the particular value system of the country. They are so closely intertwined with the U. S. social environment that their transferability without change to other societies is an impossibility.

One of these values is pragmatism. Young people in the United States absorb this value early in life, with most of them viewing education as preparation for earning a living, rather than for intellectual enrichment *per se.* A second value in the American credo is the egalitarian view that young people from all social strata are entitled to the opportunity for a university

* One unique feature of the study of THE PROFESSIONAL SCHOOL AND WORLD AFFAIRS has been the simultaneous examination of eight fields of professional education. This statement incorporates some of the general findings of the entire study which have implications broader than those that apply to any one professional field. It is adapted here from the more complete essay which will appear in the final volume containing all the reports in this series.

education. Elitism, whether viewed as represented by an upper social class or by an intellectual elite discovered by strenuous examinations, is not accepted as a general American value.

We also see in the professional school the U. S. penchant for packaging a standardized product—in this case a graduate who has been processed through a series of courses imparting disparate quanta of theory, knowledge, and vicarious or real experience demanded by professional standards which are usually set up by the nonacademic practitioner interested in maintaining the prestige of his field. Involved here also is the value of achievement, of getting ahead. In the U. S. professional school, as is true of other countries where certification depends upon successfully passing terminal examinations, the student—though offered some liberal arts courses—tends to concentrate on those items which he thinks relevant to the tests he must undergo. Often, later on as a practitioner, he wishes that he had devoted more time to other courses less utilitarian and more intellectually broadening.

To point out some of the unique features of the U. S. professional school is not to imply that what it stands for is now accepted without question in all university circles. There is emerging today a dramatic clash within U. S. society—both university and nonuniversity, between those who want to hold on to the time-honored university functions of imparting increasing knowledge, and others who want the university to concentrate a substantial portion of its intellectual resources in serving directly the needs of society. This is in part the result of the accelerating impact of the university and its people's skills and knowledge upon the world outside; it is also, needless to say, the result of the university's increasing dependence upon largesse from government, business and tax-exempt foundations.

The professional school, in a sense, represents the historical prototype and harbinger of this struggle, being torn as it always has been between the needs, values, and priorities of the university and those of the practicing profession. Viewed differently, some professional schools represent to a certain degree a buffer, an instrumentality by which one or more academic disciplines cope with meeting the needs of society—economics in schools of business administration, for instance, or the sciences in schools of engineering —while retaining their own center of gravity in the academic discipline.

THE INCREASED PROFESSIONALIZATION OF U. S. SOCIETY

One striking feature of the development of the United States has been the consistent increase in the number of professionals, both in absolute terms and in proportion to the labor force as a whole. In the period of 1900 to 1960, the American labor force grew by about 123 percent while the numbers in professional occupations multiplied by almost five—an increase of 485 percent.[1]

The U. S. Bureau of the Census figures for occupational trends, from which the above figures are taken, include "professional, technical and kindred" in the same category. Nevertheless, they are good indicators of change: in 1900, about one of twenty-four in the labor force was a professional; in 1960, one in nine was a professional; and the recent trends suggest that by 1966 the proportion was nearer to one in eight.

Striking shifts have occurred within the professions, as Professor Frederick Mosher points out:

> Among the slowest growers over the past sixty years have been the best established, most highly respected traditional professional fields: the doctors, the lawyers, the dentists, the architects, and the clergymen. In striking contrast are the engineers. In 1900, the engineers were, numerically at least, a minor profession. There were more than three times as many doctors; three times as many clergymen; nearly three times as many lawyers. With the dentists and architects, these traditional professions outnumbered the engineers by more than ten to one. By 1960, the statistics had more than reversed themselves. There were then 110,000 engineers more than the other five put together, and not one of these latter professions included as many as one-third the number of engineers.[2]

With this shift from the traditional to the newer professions, it is not surprising to find some changes in the nature of professional life.

First, the vast majority of professional people today are employees and not practitioners dealing with individual clients. They are organization men and women. They are compensated by a salary and not by fees. This tendency is accelerating even in law and medicine, which have been most oriented to the single client.

Second, professions find it increasingly difficult to discipline their members because of the wide variety of subspecialties which are springing up within them. Knowledge about each specialized field of study within a profession is so detailed that in general the members of a profession do not comprehend what their fellow-professionals are doing.

Third, the "learned" aspect of the profession is played down as technocratic professionals tend to dominate the scene. There is lip service to "learning" because it is part of the traditional model, but the real emphasis within the community tends to be not upon what the professional knows but how he can perform expected services.

Fourth, the commercialization of the profession is occurring on a widespread scale. Formerly the traditional, learned professions had an Olympian quality derived in part from their dedication to service—the requirement that the interest of the client be placed above that of the practitioner. More and more, professional people are descending from Mount Olympus to the market place. In this respect, the professions are taking on the coloration of American life.

These developments in the professionalization of American life quite clearly affect the relationship between the profession itself and the professional school which prepares future practitioners; they also affect the school's approach to international involvement.

THE INTERNATIONALIZATION OF THE PROFESSIONS

The major professions treated in this study developed in the Euro-American context. They arose to meet specific problems that individuals in the Western societies experienced. Some of them, such as medicine, deal with conditions generic to man wherever found; others, such as business administration, have grown out of the matrix of the capitalistic or free enterprise system and may need adaptations before acceptance in some other countries. Agriculture is of course worldwide, but the scientific pursuit of agricultural productivity is Western, as is the attempt to develop a research and professional establishment devoted to the spread of good agricultural practices.

But most professional fields are tending to lose their strictly national character. A number of factors are responsible for this.

Practice is becoming internationalized. Lawyers, who never expected to be concerned with international problems in their U. S. domestic practice, find that many cases which they handle have aspects involving the laws or legal systems of other countries; business administrators confront the economic and financial procedures and policies of other countries as they plot the future growth of the U. S. corporation for which they have responsibility; educators find the public increasingly comparing our school system and its products with systems and graduates from abroad, and questioning what we do. With increased international travel, practitioners from different countries come into contact and seek to understand the variations in practice which prevail in other parts of the world. The professional school graduate today is stepping into a practitioner role that is less parochial, less regional, and more national and international with every passing year.

Knowledge respects no political frontiers. Discoveries in method or in principle spread from the country of origin to other countries. Where relevant, they become incorporated in the systematized body of professional knowledge. Even in an earlier period when professional practice was pointed specifically toward serving national or more restricted ends, it was based on knowledge and discoveries from many countries and past ages. This is much more true today. In fact, great sums are expended in many fields to abstract professional literature from around the world so that its benefits can be made available to practitioners and researchers who can use this new information.

This means that there is a large increase in the amount of material to be mastered by each succeeding generation of professional school students; it also requires an ability by the wide-awake practitioner to keep in touch through the means available to him (abstracts, conferences, etc.) with what those with similar professional interests are doing elsewhere.

Many of our traditional professional school courses, reputedly "covering" a subject, are at best giving a distorted, limited view of that subject because they fail to include much relevant knowledge from non-U. S. experience. Likewise, some curricula are biased in that a student completing them is intellectually prepared for a world which existed twenty years ago and not for one twenty years hence. Particularly troublesome to each field is the definition and content of an international component such as international business, comparative education, international law, international agriculture or international health. No matter how a professional school defines its international component—as mere labels or as genuinely substantive areas—the problem of organizing and transmitting the expanding professional knowledge from many parts of the world grows more complex every year.

Students are trained in professional schools outside their own countries. Americans used to go to Europe for advanced training; now the United States is the Mecca for many graduate students from other lands. The number of foreign students in the United States has risen from 9,643 in 1930 to 82,709 in 1966, and has increased at just about twice the rate that the U. S. college enrollment itself has expanded. In addition, the percentage of those foreign students studying at the graduate level has risen from 36 to 43 percent of the total. This means that these foreign students who return to their own countries will take with them the Western-oriented characteristics of the professions they have pursued here. In one way, the process might be viewed as tending to internationalize professional practice. In another way, it may serve to perpetuate a worldwide uniformity of Western-dominated professional patterns which may be maladaptive in other cultural and economic settings, particularly in developing nations.

There is an increased emphasis upon principles and problem-solving in contrast to the earlier preoccupation with techniques. This reflects the dynamic nature of technology, for the machines and complicated techniques one masters in professional school are often out of date a few years hence. But the principles do remain. The same observation holds for a professional trying to apply his knowledge to widely varying cultures or even to quite different types of people within a single culture. This shift in emphasis does not essentially denigrate techniques which the new professional must have if he is to operate successfully. But it does give him an ability to modify techniques as occasion requires. As professions become increasingly internationalized, the importance of principles and problem-solving will grow.

Basic principles are not culture-bound, but a specific technique may very well be.

International accreditation and licensing schemes, though embryonic, are under discussion by various international bodies. These occur, for instance, when employing or licensing agencies in a country accept training in another country as satisfying the same conditions as training in the host country. This may proceed without the mediation of any international body, but there are periodic international meetings where efforts are made to work out comparable training and licensing arrangements. Licensing systems remain, as they probably should, under the control of national or subnational (e.g. State) authorities. These, in turn, can recognize the license granted by other national bodies without in any way limiting their power of action. For its own self-protection, however, a professional body in a given country must be informed about the standards set by other countries if it is to know how to deal with the migrating professionals arriving on its own shores and seeking full-fledged acceptance.

International professional associations are on the increase. The international association, both by member composition and goals, is seeking to advance on a worldwide scale the agreed-upon interests of the profession. Some of its functions are quite simple. An international body in public administration, for instance, may provide practitioners from various countries with an occasional forum to air their views and to learn what is going on in other lands; it may publish a periodical which seeks to stress common unities within the profession and to portray some of the most famous practitioners as models to be emulated; it may encourage and find financing for comparative research into the practice of the profession in different national settings; or it may seek to acquaint governmental leaders in various countries with the characteristics of the profession.

A simple listing of international meetings attended by faculty members of leading professional schools would underline the extent of such international associations and the cross-national intellectual collaboration which results.

Programs in technical cooperation increasingly involve the professional schools. These call for an interaction between the school in the United States (or other Western countries) and the school in the host country, extending oftentimes to the whole educational enterprise. Such programs have involved thousands of faculty members of U. S. professional schools, for instance, and they have returned to their campuses with a new understanding for the problems encountered by fellow-professionals in another part of the world. The same is true for the professionals in the developing country who are also afforded the opportunity, sometimes in large numbers, to pursue their study abroad. Such faculty interchange often leads to productive arrangements between U. S. universities and those in other countries.

THE PROFESSIONAL SCHOOL AND ITS UNIVERSITY

Cooperative Arrangements on a Single Campus

The U. S. professional school is learning the hard way, by trial and error, that it cannot effectively "go it alone" in its international activities. It depends upon other units of its own university for scarce talent and—in the case of overseas programs—all too often upon other schools in the same professional field for staffing. At the same time, the central university administration is learning that international programs provide the basis for all-university patterns of cooperation which bring together units that in the past had no recognized common cause.

These two conclusions on the part of the professional school and the central administration derive from the same set of facts. First, world affairs activities by their very nature cannot be logically or substantively restricted to any department, school or college. No one can claim a traditional monopoly over the field. Second, from a practical standpoint, as already indicated, any single professional school trying to give genuine international substance to its curriculum, or trying to strengthen a professional school abroad, needs additional resources from outside. Even the strongest professional schools are not really self-sufficient in international matters. Third, if there is to be any benefit to the university from the international involvement of a professional school, the results of this involvement must be fed back not only to the school itself but to the other parts of the university (e.g., area studies programs) where the results are likely to be as relevant as to the school which is originally involved. This is so because lessons learned in international activities do not restrict themselves neatly to the organizational chart of an American university. Finally, there is the tedious task of negotiating contracts or grants, of working out overseas staff and research arrangements, and financing an array of items not ordinarily a part of the U. S. academic fiscal scene. While the professional school staff needs to concern itself with many specific details of any overseas involvement, the central university administration is often able to negotiate the general provisions more effectively with the sponsoring or granting agency.

The Overall University Commitment

The continuing internationalization of contemporary U. S. academic life, in comparison with the situation before World War II, is especially evident on those campuses where the growth of area studies has brought with it a stream of foreign visitors, where the research interests of a significant number of faculty members have shifted to topics requiring study abroad, and where the university as a whole, or one or more of its professional schools, has undertaken an overseas technical cooperation contract. It is evidenced, too, by the increase in foreign students, stressed in each report of this study.

The rationale for this investment of U. S. educational resources, of both personnel and finances, has been well expressed by Charles Frankel, Assistant Secretary of State for Educational and Cultural Affairs, who maintains that U. S. education has an international responsibility whether it makes any conscious decision to fulfill that responsibility or not. He cites three reasons for this. First, the very materials of education today are international. Science is international. To an increasing extent, literature and the arts are produced for an international audience and are responses to problems whose major elements are common to many nations. Second, the world beyond our borders has become for most of us the world that is on our minds a good part of the time. To fail to register this fact in the education provided the young is to inject unreality into education—an unreality the young will recognize. Third, education is emerging progressively as the indispensable ingredient in the complex and painful process to which we have given the bland name of "economic and social development." This is not principally a material process, Mr. Frankel holds, but a psychological process, a moral transformation, dependent on education as the main hope.[3]

A university commitment shows up in many forms: the concern of the top administration for international matters as revealed in trips abroad, speeches made, guests invited to the university, and—most important of all—a readiness to seek funds in support of international programs. Many institutions have formalized this commitment in one of several ways. They have appointed a Dean or Director of International Programs or they have set up a Center for International Studies. These may have the mandate to try to coordinate various programs, to suggest new dimensions to be considered, and to help faculty members and schools find the resources for new ideas they wish to carry out. These deans and directors usually work with a representative committee drawn from across the campus and increasingly with associate directors located in those schools which have very active international programs.[4]

Several universities prominent in developing international interests have taken a further step: they have prepared an all-university plan covering the next five or ten years. This is based on the goals set by each department, school and college, on an analysis of existing resources, and on a strategy for implementing those items in the plan which are given top priority for the university as a whole. For a professional school such a plan has certain marked advantages: first, as a unit of the whole it has had to decide for itself as part of the planning process whether it wishes to expand its involvement in international matters, and, if so, in what ways; second, the plan helps the school discover what other units in the university have similar interests, often leading to productive joint appointments and joint research projects; third, when the school does explore the possibilities of outside support from a foundation or a government agency, it can show how its own proposals fit into the total university effort. This gives the funding agency a greater assurance of continuity than if the request seemed to be an *ad hoc*, one-time affair.

Experience shows, however, that the all-university arrangements can help but are no substitute for the very hard work that must be done within the professional school itself if there is to be genuine course enrichment, a better-trained faculty, a research program that makes faculty and student more keenly aware of the international aspects of their profession, and a readiness to serve abroad where this helps to carry out the goals identified by the school.

IRWIN T. SANDERS,
Study Director

PETER N. GILLINGHAM,
Associate Study Director

Notes

[1] From unpublished manuscript of Frederick C. Mosher entitled "The Professions, Professional Education, and the Public Service," to be published in 1967 or 1968 by the Chandler Publishing Company.

[2] *Ibid.*

[3] "Education for World Responsibility: An Old Phrase, a Transformed Problem," excerpts from an address delivered at The National Foreign Policy Conference for Educators, Washington D.C., June 16-17, 1966, reprinted in a special issue of the *Department of State Bulletin*, Vol. 55, July 18, 1966, pp. 84-85.

[4] See *The University Looks Abroad: Approaches to World Affairs at Six American Universities*, New York: Walker & Co. (for Education and World Affairs), 1966.

TASK FORCES

Agriculture and Engineering

Paul A. Miller, Task Force Chairman   Assistant Secretary for Education, Department of Health, Education, and Welfare

Paul F. Chenea   Vice President for Academic Affairs, Purdue University

D. W. Colvard   Chancellor, University of North Carolina at Charlotte

Thomas F. Jones, Jr.   President, University of South Carolina

Frederick C. Lindvall   Chairman, Division of Engineering and Applied Science, California Institute of Technology

Erven J. Long   Director, AID Research and Institutional Grants, Agency for International Development

William R. Pritchard   Dean, School of Veterinary Medicine, University of California, Davis

Louis N. Wise   Vice President for Agriculture and Forestry, Mississippi State University

David C. Nichols, Task Force Assistant   Office of the Assistant Secretary for Education, Department of Health, Education, and Welfare

Business Administration and Public Administration

Albert C. Van Dusen, Task Force Chairman   Vice Chancellor—The Professions, University of Pittsburgh

Stephen K. Bailey   Dean, Maxwell Graduate School of Citizenship and Public Affairs, Syracuse University

Robert C. Calkins   President, The Brookings Institution

John J. Corson   Consultant

C. Jackson Grayson, Jr.   Dean, School of Business Administration, Tulane University

Henry Reining, Jr.   Dean, School of Public Administration, University of Southern California

Alvin Roseman   Associate Dean, Graduate School of Public and International Affairs, University of Pittsburgh

George P. Shultz   Dean, Graduate School of Business, University of Chicago

Ralph H. Smuckler   Acting Dean of International Programs, Michigan State University

Education and Law

Edward H. Levi, Task Force Chairman   Provost, University of Chicago

Derek C. Bok   Professor, Harvard University Law School

John H. Fischer   President, Teachers College, Columbia University

Fowler Hamilton   Cleary, Gottlieb, Steen & Hamilton, New York

Frank C. Newman   Professor, School of Law, University of California, Berkeley

I. James Quillen   Professor, School of Education, Stanford University

Lindley J. Stiles   Professor, School of Education, Northwestern University

Peter Karasz, Task Force Assistant   Fellow in International Trade and Development, University of Chicago Law School

Medicine and Public Health

Mark H. Lepper, M.D., Task Force Chairman   Executive Vice President, Professional and Academic Affairs, Presbyterian-St. Luke's Hospital, Chicago

Ivan L. Bennett, Jr., M.D.   Deputy Director, Office of Science and Technology, Executive Office of the President

Leroy E. Burney, M.D.   Vice President for Health Sciences, Temple University

George T. Harrell, Jr., M.D.   Dean, College of Medicine, The Milton S. Hershey Medical Center, The Pennsylvania State University

Richard K. C. Lee, M.D.   Director, Public Health and Medical Activities, Department of Public Health, University of Hawaii

William D. Lotspeich, M.D.   Chairman, Department of Physiology, School of Medicine and Dentistry, University of Rochester

Kenneth W. Newell, M.D.   Acting Director, Division of Hygiene and Tropical Medicine, School of Medicine, Tulane University

John M. Dowd, M.D. Task Force Assistant   Assistant Professor, College of Medicine, University of Illinois Medical Center

Consultants

James L. Troupin, M.D.   Director of Professional Education, American Public Health Association

Henry van Zile Hyde, M.D.   Director, Division of International Medical Education, Association of American Medical Colleges

Publications

Studies and reports issued by Education and World Affairs:

AID and the Universities, by John W. Gardner. Published by Education and World Affairs, 1964.

The U. S. Office of Education: A New International Dimension. Published by Education and World Affairs, 1964.

The Foreign Student: Whom Shall We Welcome? Published by Education and World Affairs, 1964. (Out of print.)

The University Looks Abroad: Approaches to World Affairs at Six American Universities. Published by Walker & Company for Education and World Affairs, 1966.

The Overseas Selection of Foreign Students. Published by Education and World Affairs, 1966.

The following publications and information services have been provided by Education and World Affairs:

Education and World Affairs: Report on Program 1963-1964. Published by Education and World Affairs, 1965.

Intercultural Education. Published by Education and World Affairs, 1965. (Out of print.)

International Education Program, 1966. Published by Education and World Affairs, 1966. (Out of print.)

Education and World Affairs: An Overview. Published by Education and World Affairs, 1966. (Out of print.)

As Nations Become Neighbors. Reprinted from *Saturday Review*, August 20, 1966 issue.

The International Education Act of 1966. Published by Education and World Affairs, 1966.

Coordinating International Programs and Activities at U. S. Colleges and Universities: A Directory. Published by Education and World Affairs, 1966.

Occasional Reports:

No. 1. The Teaching of Economics in Mexico, by Blanca M. de Petricioli and Clark Winton Reynolds. Published by Education and World Affairs, 1967.

No. 2. Guidelines for the Planning of External Aid Projects in Education, by Arthur J. Lewis. Published by Education and World Affairs, 1967.

No. 3. Scientific, Engineering and Technical Education in Mexico, by Russell G. Davis. Published by Education and World Affairs, 1967.

Policy Statements:

The University Community and Overseas Research: Guidelines for the Future. Board of Trustees of Education and World Affairs, 1967.

In addition to these reports, several other publications are distributed by EWA.

The University and World Affairs. Report of the Committee on the University and World Affairs, J. L. Morrill, chairman. Published by the Ford Foundation, 1960.

The College and World Affairs. Report of the Committee on the College and World Affairs, John W. Nason, chairman. Published by the Hazen Foundation, 1964.

Some Facts about Serving in Educational Posts Abroad. Published by Overseas Educational Service, 1964.

Overseas Educational Service: Its Purpose and Program. Published by Overseas Educational Service, 1965.

EDUCATION AND WORLD AFFAIRS

Education and World Affairs is a private, nonprofit educational organization created in 1962 to study, analyze and assist in strengthening the international teaching, research and service dimensions of U. S. colleges and universities. Its priorities and approaches are determined by its Board of Trustees and are based on continuous consultations with American universities and colleges and many other private groups as well as with United States governmental agencies. EWA draws its basic support from grants of the Ford Foundation and the Carnegie Corporation of New York.

The views expressed in its publications are those of Education and World Affairs itself, its study committees, or individual authors, as the case may be. They are not necessarily the views of the foundations and other donors whose funds support the organization's work.